A man comes across an ancient enemy, beaten and left for dead. He lifts the wounded man onto the back of a donkey and takes him to an inn to tend to the man's recovery. Jesus tells this story and instructs those who are listening to "go and do likewise."

Likewise books explore a compassionate, active faith lived out in real time. When we're skeptical about the status quo, Likewise books challenge us to create culture responsibly. When we're confused about who we are and what we're supposed to be doing, Likewise books help us listen for God's voice. When we're discouraged by the troubled world we've inherited, Likewise books encourage us to hold onto hope.

In this life we will face challenges that demand our response. Likewise books face those challenges with us so we can act in faith.

LIKE

2007

PRACTICAL
JUSTICE

LIVING OFF-CENTER IN
A SELF-CENTERED WORLD

KEVIN BLUE

IVP Books

An imprint of InterVarsity Press
Downers Grove, Illinois

InterVarsity Press
P.O. Box 1400, Downers Grove, IL 60515-1426
World Wide Web: www.ivpress.com
E-mail: email@ivpress.com

InterVarsity Press® is the book-publishing division of InterVarsity Christian Fellowship/USA®, a student movement active on campus at hundreds of universities, colleges and schools of nursing in the United States of America, and a member movement of the International Fellowship of Evangelical Students. For information about local and regional activities, write Public Relations Dept., InterVarsity Christian Fellowship/USA, 6400 Schroeder Rd., P.O. Box 7895, Madison, WI 53707-7895, or visit the IVCF website at <www.intervarsity.org>.

The Scripture quotations quoted herein are from the Revised Standard Version of the Bible, copyright 1946, 1952, 1971 by the Division of Christian Education of the National Council of the Churches of Christ in the U.S.A. Used by permission. All rights reserved.

Quote on pages 75-77 is from Savage Inequalities by Jonathan Kozol, copyright © 1991 by Jonathan Kozol. Used by permission of Crown Publishers, a division of Random House, Inc.

Every effort has been made to contact copyright holders for materials quoted in this book. The author will be pleased to rectify any omissions in future editions if notified by copyright holders.

Design: Cindy Kiple
Images: Ian Shaw/Getty Images

ISBN-10: 0-8308-3368-4
ISBN-13: 978-0-8308-3368-9

Printed in the United States of America ∞

Library of Congress Cataloging-in-Publication Data
Blue, Kevin.
    Practical justice: living off-center in a self-centered world/
    Kevin Blue.
      p. cm.
    ISBN-13: 978-0-8308-3368-9 (pbk.: alk. paper)
    ISBN-10: 0-8308-3368-4 (pbk.: alk. paper)
    A. Christian life. I. Title.
    BV4501.3.B58 2006
    261.8—dc22

                                             2006030080

P	20	19	18	17	16	15	14	13	12	11	10	9	8	7	6	5	4	3	2
Y	23	22	21	20	19	18	17	16	15	14	13	12	11	10	09	08	07		

To Philip Butcher

*May the gifts given to the family
continue to be passed down the
generations.*

CONTENTS

INTRODUCTION

GETTING YOUR HOUSE IN ORDER

AS LONG AS I CAN REMEMBER, whenever I have heard Martin Luther King Jr.'s voice I have been compelled to listen. I have been unable to simply continue whatever I had been doing. One time, as I was walking up the stairs, a TV program began airing one of his speeches. After a while I realized that I had just stopped and was standing there, listening. Something about his words had such potency; something in them was inescapably real. Though by now I have heard some of his speeches many times, I am still drawn to quietness in the presence of those words.

I was first introduced to Jesus in the ninth grade. I attended a private school, and though the curriculum did not demand Christian faith, it did require that we study the Old and New Testaments with some thoroughness. My teacher was Mr. Starr, and over the course of the first semester I was captured by the Jesus he introduced me to in the Gospel accounts. I had read some of the stories before and had heard them in Sunday school since before I could remember. But here I felt I was seeing Jesus really for the first time.

To my surprise, it turned out that Jesus was a man of passion. He turned over the tables of a group of men handling currency exchange to confront a corrupt religious and economic system. He hung out with the ordinary people of his day and chose them to be his most trusted friends. He noticed and spent time with people who were hurting, diseased, the kind of people who were unwelcome in polite society. He cared for those who were in need, and he called everybody to change their ways and co-operate with the government of God. He spent time with those who were considered sell-outs. And he taught with a sharpness, a clarity and a boldness that drew people to listen. He was provocative, dramatic, even sarcastic at times. He was a powerful voice for the way things should be in his time. He was such a threat to the people of power in his time that though he posed no threat of violence, they put him to death.

Before this experience, Jesus had seemed a bit dull to me—sort of blurred in all the grays of tame mediocrity. But now all of a sudden he was in full color, and I could hardly stop thinking about what I had seen. I was drawn to him, what his life was about, what he taught and how he taught it, what he did and how he did it. It was an amazing experience.

Not until my freshman year of college did I encounter this Jesus again; and to be honest, I had missed him. In between those times, I sat through a lot of sermons and Sunday schools, and many things we talked about in church didn't seem to matter much. It's still that way sometimes. The same Spirit of God that compelled Dr. King to preach and Mr. Starr to teach now compelled me to listen closely to Jesus' words. Jesus' life, and particularly his words, became powerful to me. King's dream was first Jesus' dream—Dr. King had simply applied it to his generation. Since this discovery, I continue to be drawn into quiet-ness in the presence of Jesus' word.

THE DEBATE

Since I began following Jesus in a deliberate manner during my college years, I have found some discussions about the Bible frustrating. There has been a great deal of national and international debate and division concerning the place of evangelism and social concern. Some churches seem to focus so little on the social dimensions of the gospel, and others focus on those dimensions exclusively. Some call us to personal righteousness but have little to say about social or corporate righteousness. Some want to talk about evangelism and sharing the good news but have nothing to say about concerns of substantive justice for individuals or groups. The dichotomy can be maddening for people who are awake to both what is happening in the world around us and the Jesus I met many years ago now.

I grew up in a church context that spoke little about social concern but in a family that was keenly aware of social issues. As a young man, I was taught by my parents to respond slowly and carefully when a police officer stops you. I heard my family's stories about the segregated conditions they grew up in. I knew about some of my ancestors and their slavery in Virginia. We talked about the racial and class inequities in the United States and how some members of our family had been the first to make headway socially or economically in some profession. I learned certain parts of American history that were not included in school textbooks but were addressed in family letters and stories that had been passed down.

As I grew older, I learned more about injustice in society. I saw the homeless population explode as many mentally ill people were released onto the streets. I saw racial tension in the streets and in school. Some friends and I were threatened by a bunch of white guys at football games. There were racial slurs periodically. Yet in church we never even talked about race. Where was God in all this? What had happened to the Jesus I had met in ninth grade? What did the church have to do with these real issues?

Such questions rumbled around in me as I grew older, and only in college did I find the blended spirituality that the Scriptures commend to us and that Jesus demonstrated through his life. We are to be about both sharing the good news in word and living out our faith in good works, which express social concern.

Since then, God has called me to be a part of various Christian movements and churches, most of them strongly evangelical. I have still found few communities that seem to integrate these elements of the gospel well. And until relatively recently, I've found little substantive concern for justice issues. So if you are concerned for justice and desire to understand how we might make this passion a central part of our Christian spirituality, you and I are on the same journey. But before I go on, let me tell you how I really feel about things.

GETTING OUR HOUSE IN ORDER

I have come to believe that the purpose of the church includes a mandate to care for the poor and to be involved in substantive justice work. We are to be Jesus' body, ministering to a world gone mad, with a particular concern for the poor.

As is always the case in following Jesus, as we do what he has instructed, we discover more of who he is and what he is doing in us and through us. We are changed as we hope for and pray for change in others and in society around us. We are called to be God's reminder to those who suffer in poverty and injustice that he has not forgotten about them. We are the physical expression of his love for them, his compassion and his desire to be with them. We are directly commanded in Scripture to have this type of presence, this type of ministry. We are to have a particular concern for the poor and needy in the world, those people without a voice, without power and without options. This concern is, as my book's subtitle suggests, off-center in a self-centered world.

This is not an issue just for the West or the United States, nor is it an issue only for wealthy believers. It is part of the ministry and purpose of the church across the board, regardless of economic status and area of the world. We are to be in solidarity, together, in this kind of ministry.

Yet I have found a curious thing in my years of following Jesus in the United States. Is it not curious that we spend so much of our church budgets on things that are simply not commanded in Scripture? Why is this? Countless (OK, hundreds) of passages in the Old and New Testaments directly command us to minister to the needs of the poor. We are commanded to spread the good news of the gospel to every people group, in every corner of the world. We are even commanded to support the work of those missionaries who do such things—who go on behalf of all of us who stay. And yet so much of our budget is consumed with the building fund, or building upkeep, or high-tech gadgets, or the band, or the organ—billions of dollars every single year. All of this for a God who says he will not dwell in a house made by human hands. How is it that we can spend millions of dollars on a new cathedral in a city where people have problems finding food to eat, clothes to wear and places to sleep? Now that is depressing. My brothers and sisters, this should not be so.

Surely it is not necessarily a problem to have a building or musical instruments. But it might be, and given our culture's seductive materialism and consumerism combined with the love of wealth, we should be *very* careful.

Personally, I am tired of the needless debates that have raged in the church in recent decades. Believers have argued and continue to argue about whether the gospel actually includes social action or is just about verbal evangelism and the saving of souls. Thankfully, in recent years there have been interdenominational movements that have affirmed that the gospel is about both. The Gospels show the Lord ministering to those in need as he taught about the kingdom of God. Ministering to those in need is not the whole gospel. Talking about the kingdom alone is equally pathetic. Scripture itself offers that the kingdom of God is not about mere talk (see 1 Corinthians 4:20). At the same time, social concern alone is an emaciated representation of what the healthy body of Christ should look like in action. Loving the poor is a demonstration of the gospel and is commended in many parts of the Bible, but this should be coupled with verbal witness, as the Scripture demonstrates.

The gospel has flourished in many countries. It has become a fire in many places around the world. And it has, through the generations, been a source of social transformation. The kingdom of God is about many things. It is about forgiveness; it is about character transformation; it is about purity in sexual relations; it is about compassion for those in need; it is about healing; it is about declaring and demonstrating the good news to those who don't yet know.

Let us never throw out that which is ours by design. We have been given no right to renegotiate the terms on which we will follow Christ. Nor have we been given the right to rewrite our marching orders—our constitution if you will. This is not a democracy where we can change the basics through a majority vote. The believing community is actually a monarchy—and there will always be but one King. Given this, we must receive whatever (and whoever) he says is part of his kingdom—no exceptions.

We may struggle, for such is our human condition and such is the testimony of the disciples who came before us. Even Peter, whom Jesus called the great rock of the church, the leader of the church in Jerusalem, struggled as he followed. Both before and after Pentecost he fought with his preconceived notions of what the kingdom and the gospel and Jesus were about. But God did not let him define the faith in whatever way he wanted. Jesus and his Spirit continued to work in Peter, as the Gospels and Acts record, to make him accept the full picture—without exceptions. Should we expect to have it easier than Peter did?

Peter's longest struggle was with the ethnic inclusiveness of the gospel. This is a major struggle in our day as well, though I will not address it in this book. Another of our difficulties is with our responsibility to those in need. The issue is holism: we should be concerned with the whole package, the whole gospel, and not just one or a couple of aspects of the faith.

In our day, how do we address the lack of concern for substantive justice and righteousness in the church, beyond certain popular public topics? What does it mean to *be* the message and not simply say it? It is my sincere hope that we shall come to terms with the whole of the gospel and see the kind of revival that many of us long for in the West. Indeed believers in other parts of the world long for a revival among us here, for they (more so than us) feel our shortcomings. And thus, with the encouragement of friends, I have written this exploration of what it will mean for us to take seriously Scripture's call to justice, righteousness and concern for the poor.

A FEW NOTES ABOUT THE REST OF THE BOOK

Urban issues. Our world is becoming more and more urban, and at an alarming rate. This is true of people in general, but particularly true of people living in poverty. Poverty is thus becoming increasingly urban. For this reason, I believe we must focus on issues surrounding the urban poor. Poverty in less urban areas still needs to be addressed. But in this book, I will focus largely on poverty's urban face.

My point is not that every Christian needs to be living among the urban poor to minister the gospel. Some believers *should* be there, but there are plenty of places where a concern for the poor needs to take root. God will lead us where we need to be, and wherever we are, a concern for those in need should be a part of our spirituality.

Wealth issues. As you read the book, please keep in mind that when I speak of the community of faith, I mean both those who have substantial material resources and education and those who have little. The biblical command to be people of justice who have a concern for the poor is not addressed only to the wealthy. It is a command to the church. There is no room for class divisions in this discussion. God's people are to be concerned for the poor and seek to be of service. This will look different depending on what community of faith we are involved with and what resources we bring to the table, but all of us are to be committed together in ministering to those the world overlooks.

Furthermore, in regard to the call to care for the poor, I make no distinction between those who are in need who are believers and those who are not. Certainly the Bible tells us that we are to care for those in the community of faith. But we are also encouraged to love and care for *all* those in need. For the purposes of this discussion, I will make no effort to distinguish between these groups.

Style issues. The book includes sections that have a teaching orientation and others with a more sermonic, preaching tone. To be honest, I find writing very frustrating because it is too stagnant. I cannot see the congregation, explain something further or interact about an idea with anyone. I prefer discussions in person.

You as a reader may be accustomed to an analytical, deliberate, nuanced teaching tone in literature and conversation. Or you may be refreshed by a more combative, prophetic, direct, impassioned oratorical tone in written work and preaching. In this book you will find both. I encourage you to let the different tones of writing be a sort of cross-cultural experience as the discussion develops. I speak and write in both styles.

The following pages invite you on a tour through some of the passages I have found helpful, as well as through some reflections on society. Chapters addressing the biblical basis for ministry that involves concern for the poor lead into an examination of the varied categories of justice ministry and how they work together. Finally, a few chapters look at some of the difficulties we will face and provide counsel about maintaining spiritual integrity. Stories, examples and ideas are integrated throughout.

At times I am critical of what I see in the Western church. But Martin Luther King Jr.'s eloquent words explain this better than I could on my own: "In deep disappointment, I have wept over the laxity of the church. But be assured, my tears have been tears of love. There can be no deep disappointment where there is not deep love" ("A Testament of Hope," in *Letter from a Birmingham Jail*, p. 299). I too love the church. I too have wept. I too hope to see and live rightly in our times. It is out of concern for all of us that I write these things.

God is working. I simply hope for more and write toward that end. And though these matters can and must be discussed in civil tones, they also merit sharp words, passionate words.

May God pour out his cleansing fire on us again and set us on the proper course. I pray it be so.

1

GOD'S FORGOTTEN ONES

ONE SUMMER, Johnny was ministering among the poor on a six-week urban project with InterVarsity Christian Fellowship in Los Angeles. Part of his assignment was to spend time in a convalescent home in the central part of the city. The elderly who are in need make up a segment of the poor who are easily overlooked in our society. Since many are tucked away in homes and hospices, they are not as visible as are those who are younger and on the streets.

This convalescent home was smelly, understaffed and poorly kept. Few residents had visitors. For a new guest arriving to serve the residents, it was very awkward. Some residents were mentally ill; some were not responsive at all. Others were even hostile. Members of Johnny's team were struggling in the first few days with why they had been called to serve there. "Why are we here?" "This is depressing." "We can't do anything to help." Such remarks began to be made openly.

One day, after Johnny had been there for about a week, an elderly woman slowly walked up to him in the hallway where he was standing. She drew close and pointed a finger at him. "I know why you're here," she said in an accusatory tone.

She paused as my friend looked at her, wondering what this was about. Realizing he didn't know what she meant, she went on. "I know why you're here," she said again. "You're here because God wants us to know he hasn't forgotten about us."

The woman turned and shuffled away. Johnny was stunned. Another team member was so moved she nearly cried on the spot. By the end of that summer, many of that team cried as they left the friends they had made, because in many of those relationships they had found something of the kingdom of God.

In that moment, the person who spoke to Johnny that first week was not a delirious old woman but a prophet who saw the kingdom of God with a sharpness that he could not imagine. With one line she had indeed summarized one of the central purposes of God in bringing him to visit with the residents. Johnny would have taken paragraphs to explain this purpose, fumbling through Christian words and concepts. But a little old lady, poor in means, alone in a convalescent home, could see and sense the work of God more deeply and sharply than anyone on his team. She had received the word of the Lord, in the flesh—the incarnate love of God in the team that visited her that summer. It was a beautiful moment, one that Johnny will never forget.

As my friend found out that summer, many of those in need have God-given dignity and insight. The Lord's wisdom may be found there. In fact, the Lord himself is found among the poor. The kingdom of God is found in the dirty, grimy, common places of the world. And in his presence, we are all changed.

This was another central purpose in bringing Johnny and the other students to be with the elderly in this convalescent home over the summer. Jesus wanted them to know him and to know his work among those who are in need. For them, the point that summer was not so much that they came to help the elderly remember that God hadn't forgotten them. That was the Lord's word to the woman and to her friends in that place. The word to Johnny was a bit different. It was as though God said, "I have seen and remember these people who live here, in need and out of sight. I have not forgotten them. Have you?" That was a word that Johnny and all of us involved in that summer's urban project heard loud and clear.

But through his experience at the convalescent home, Johnny also heard a more subtle word—an invitation to him. It was as though Jesus said, "Come meet me here, among these people."

This is the unique experience of those who minister among the poor. They are invited to encounter the utterly beautiful presence of God in the midst of those in need. It is mystical; it is difficult to describe. But the experience is known to many of God's people. Mother Teresa and St. Francis had the experience; and the invitation is extended to all of God's people when we receive the good news of Jesus and decide to follow him.

In the sheep and goats story at the end of Matthew 25, Jesus says that inasmuch as we have helped those who are poor and outcast, we have ministered to him. He so identifies with those who are in need that as we serve them, Jesus tells us, we encounter *him*. It is this meeting, this encountering of Jesus and his good news that so many people of his day found so disturbing.

A DISTURBING DIAMOND

The good news that Jesus brought about the reign of God involves many things. A good friend of mine once asked, "What is the gospel?" and many people responded with something like "The gospel is the good news that God sent Jesus to die for our sins and reconcile us to himself." But when does Jesus say that this is all the gospel is? He offers that to know him is eternal life (John 17:3). John 3:16 is usually attributed to Jesus, and so maybe we can say that in one sermon he defined the gospel as his death for our reconciliation.

But Scripture tells us that at the beginning of Jesus' ministry he comes into Galilee preaching the gospel of God, and he says, "The time is fulfilled, and the kingdom of God is at hand; repent, and believe in the gospel" (Mark 1:15). This seems to associate the gospel with a fixed time that has now culminated (the time is fulfilled), a realized political reality (a kingdom), a radical 180-degree change in a person (repentance) and commitment (belief).

That doesn't sound quite as simple as the definition found in gospel tracts. It seems many-faceted, like a jewel, perfectly cut, glimmering with striking brilliance as the light bounces off all its intricate surfaces, producing so many colors and such exquisite beauty that viewers lose their breath. It is so compelling that, if clearly seen, any person would go out immediately and liquidate their resources in order to acquire it. It is so compelling as to disturb the course of a life. To say "It is a diamond" of this precious stone is true, but these words hardly capture its beauty, intricacy or compelling nature.

Always time conscious and aiming for efficiency, we like to come up with one-line formulas to describe the gospel. Yet in truth, Jesus preaches about so many topics with such varied analogies and object lessons that if his topic is always this gospel, then it is an amazingly involved and complex thing. It may be good news—indeed it is—but it is so involved, so all-encompassing, so demanding, so alarming, so violent and radically different in nature, that on one occasion he said that a person must be entirely re-created to receive it (see John 3:3). The person who receives this good news must simply start over and push the reset button in life.

Jesus says nothing so simple as, "Well, if you just think that I'm here to save the world, that I will die for you, then rise, and that I'll eventually come back, you'll be cool." Conversion is not a matter of intellectual assent. It is true that our minds, our very thoughts, are hostile to God and need to be transformed (Romans 12:2). We must be retrained in how to think. We must throw out all the old ways we have been taught and learn freshly from the master teacher. We must begin again. But it is not only a matter of intellectual assent, much less to a one- or two-line doctrine. *All* of us needs to be remade. We need to learn how to act right, to see right, to love right, to hate right, and we have a teacher, a counselor, who will instruct us: the Holy Spirit.

This is all very disturbing, and rightly so. No one who encountered Jesus was able to just ignore him. All went away disturbed. The person and the message they encountered in Jesus were fundamentally different from the way they were used to seeing things; it was alarming. It was good news to some. Better said, it was really good news to all, but only some received it as good news. And the gospel is just that—a beautiful, disturbing reality that God is bringing into the world.

The word *gospel* is used only fifteen times in all the Gospels combined. And none of those verses define it very clearly. In several it is referred to as the good news of the kingdom. In several it is associated with the poor—good news specifically for them. But it is used as a general term and always associated with Jesus, his coming and his ministry.

If Jesus' central concern was to distribute the good news to people, then his many sermons as recorded by Matthew, Mark, Luke and John should give us a glimpse of what that good news is (especially since it is not defined in a nutshell as we might like). The most frequent single topic in Jesus' teaching seems to be the kingdom of God. He is centrally concerned that people understand what this kingdom is about. He is concerned that they enter it, becoming citizens of his realm. This is the goal of his ministry: whether he is healing people or casting out demons or speaking to a crowd, his central concern is that people enter the kingdom of God.

HOW GOOD DOES THE GOOD NEWS SOUND?

This kingdom of God, which is supposed to be good news particularly to the poor, is not well received by everyone. It is true that before Jesus' trial and death, many people followed him. But these were mostly common people. They were the poor, the blue-collar workers, not the economically or socially elite, not the politically powerful. The faith, the kingdom, the gospel that Jesus preached did not generally seem to be heard by such people as good news. A few prominent people did follow him and receive his teaching as good news. But many others viewed it as such a threat, such a revolutionary and even destructive force, that they killed him for it. It was not good news to them. They could not see the good in it.

Down through ensuing generations of humanity, the true gospel has never been popular among those who have found great success in the world. Only in some moments of rousing revival have many of those who have worldly privileges really renounced their other allegiances and followed only God. The "gospel" that has been popular is a version that allows and commands no substantive change in the way we live, think and relate.

In the United States today, divorce rates, sexual practices and consumer lifestyle choices are largely the same for those who claim Christian faith and those who do not. Few are disturbed by the "gospels" that are commonly preached, for these syncretistic versions of the Christian faith have been co-opted by our world of idols. Love of money, individualism, materialism and consumerism have polluted our Christian spirituality. This gospel tells us that if we only believe, we will be materially wealthy, in good health, masters of our economic future and able to live the high life. Then there is the pop-psychology, self-fulfillment, achievement-oriented version, which tells us if we only believe, we will be happy, stable and healed, without a care in the world. This cannot be the same gospel that Jesus preached.

These versions don't match up well with the economic hardship, substantial persecution, and real pain and suffering that the New Testament church underwent. When sin is repented of, people's economic circumstances do often improve, and in the presence of God there is joy and healing. Yet these blessings must be placed in clear balance with the rest of the teaching and lifestyle of the gospel.

A COUNTERFEIT VISION?

Frequently what we have instead of Jesus' good news is news that is good for allowing us to continue to do as we please. It is good news for just us. It is not good news for the poor, since we have the habit of supporting economic policies (domestic and international) that exploit the poor for our benefit. It is not about entering God's kingdom through great difficulty and suffering, since many of our habits and strategies aim toward making ourselves comfortable. It is not about hating one's own life or about living simply, since we indulge freely in self-realization groups and the pursuit of riches. It can't be about making a choice of allegiances between the state, our own family and God since we are rarely forced to make these hard choices. Though Jesus says the gospel is about justice for the poor, abandoning everything else for God's kingdom, and hating our lives, we frequently seem to define it otherwise. The gospel apparently has become the good news that we don't have to change and can look forward to a bright future in the world.

Yes, the kingdom of God is about evangelism: it seeks new members who desire to live under God's direction and guidance, who are willing to be retrained in life. Yes, the kingdom of God is about healing, sometimes of a very personal and emotional nature. Yes, the kingdom of God is about power—the power of God's Spirit ministering to finite people. And yes, the kingdom of God is about dealing with the evil and injustice in the world. Those who have become part of God's kingdom will speak out about injustice, even as Jesus did.

Most fundamentally for us, the kingdom of God is not just about us. It is not about justifying a lifestyle that we want to live at the expense of the rest of the world. It is not just about having an ecstatic experience that would justify the way we live and help us forget our conscience and the heart of God.

Jesus is very clear that concern for those in need is a litmus test of faith, not to be failed by any who hope to enter his kingdom. God has not forgotten about the poor. The question for us is whether we have forgotten about God.

The kingdom of God is about justice. It is about people being drawn back to worship God and choosing to act faithfully. It is about personal and corporate righteousness. It is about the justice of God, the justice that his people are to pursue by his means. It is about justice and not *just us*. This vision, the vision of shalom, is not new, but it is news. Some of us are rediscovering it in the Scriptures and in life in the church.

2

SHOULD I HELP?

THROUGH THE WAY JESUS LIVES and through his teaching, Jesus calls those who would share in his kingdom to care for those in need. We see him healing and touching lepers, feeding the hungry, caring for the sick, healing the paralyzed and raising the dead. He is moved with compassion for those who are grieving. He stops to talk with beggars, even seeking them out in the midst of many who are clamoring for his attention. He takes time to listen to social outcasts and ministers to them. It is inconvenient, and it seems inefficient. Most seminary experiences don't look like the mentoring Jesus offered.

In the midst of a limited life (about three years of public ministry, the time required to complete most M.Div. programs) and with a pressing message that had to be preached, Jesus spent time with those who were considered disposable. It was central to his work: the gospel, his good news, was to be good news to them in particular. Jesus takes this so seriously as to tell some of John the Baptist's disciples that such things are evidence of his claim that he is the one to come (Luke 7:22-23).

In his inaugural address in Luke 4, at the beginning of his public ministry, Jesus states clearly that his work is to bring good news to the poor. This concern for the poor is evidently one of the signs and wonders that distinguishes kingdom ministry from the way of the world. This of course means the *actual* poor, not the spiritually hungry as we in the West are apt to read the Luke 4 passage. We must not overspiritualize the message of Jesus to simply be about positive attitudes and hope for the hereafter. This was one of Malcolm X's trenchant critiques of the Christian faith as he saw it practiced. The faith that Jesus lived and preached is about the here and now as well as life after death.

THE STRUGGLE

"Give a man a fish and you feed him for a day. Teach him how to fish and you feed him for a lifetime. Therefore, don't give a man a fish." This is the cultural mantra of much of the middle and upper class. While Jesus says directly to give to those who ask (Matthew 5:42), we are encouraged to interview, be suspicious of and ultimately not give to beggars. Why?

It seems we think that people are poor because they ought to be. Or is it like a disease that can be caught if you associate too closely? We are taught that those who are poor don't want to work, are manipulative, don't care about themselves or others, are criminally dangerous, or are unmotivated to do better. Yet Jesus doesn't mention any of these conditions as reasons not to give to someone in need.

Truth be told, I know a fair number of people who make plenty of money of whom we should be suspicious, who should be investigated, who are pretty darn lazy and manipulative, and who care little about others. So why is there all the noise about beggars being this way? We are taught that there is abundant opportunity for all who are willing to work hard. Thus people with wealth cannot believe that we should relate with or help anyone who is poor. The poor should be able to help themselves.

I regularly hear people contend that poor people want to be poor or that it is their personal responsibility to deal with their situation. First, that is not Jesus' perspective, nor that of the Old Testament writers. While Scripture affirms personal responsibility, it also affirms our corporate responsibility to help one another. Not only that, it also recognizes that poverty can be related to various social structures that take advantage of people. Such systems are set up and maintained by the powerful to keep the poor at a disadvantage. We are not just called to charity but to work for structured, systemic change. Second, we need to take account of the profound effect that culture and its media can have on us. When we make judgments about the poor, are we speaking from our relationships with actual people in these situations? Or are our judgments based only on statistics and news stories? Personal sin and responsibility always play a part in people's hardships. However, in nearly every needy person I have known, the situation was not that simple.

One familiar caution is that we want to be sure that the money we give is used for food or another real need and not drugs. We want to be sure the recipient actually needs the money and that we have not been had, scammed, hoodwinked, bamboozled, taken—you get the idea. While it's never nice to be scammed, the overzealous expression of this concern makes me wonder about other motives. Maybe we should interview every employed person who makes more than forty thousand dollars a year and find out if they actually *need* all that money or have some wasteful habits. If they don't actually need the money, let's have them keep working and have their employer reduce their check. If we are really going to take the integrity stick out, we should use it to measure integrity all the way around. We should not disregard the way the Lord says we should invest our resources—since they are his anyway.

Now there is a difference between working for your money and receiving it as a gift from someone. At best, people give to meet a need and not to support a drug habit or a lavish lifestyle. But since all that we have is given by God, not won through our merit, is it really very different? Health, a good education, opportunities and a good job that pays well are God's gifts, and so is the dollar I give to a beggar. Both are gifts, and we must choose to use the gifts of God well and wisely. We should be wise in our giving, but let us not be fooled into not giving for fear of being fooled. God knows and sees the truth of every situation. We are not the beggar's judge: like us, she must also render an account to God.

Work is important, and Scripture teaches that all human beings were created for it. Notice that God gave us the job of tilling and keeping the garden (Genesis 2:15) and told human beings to subdue the earth and exercise dominion over it (Genesis 1:28). Work is part of the created order of things and God's intent for us. We were meant to work; work is not a result of the Fall. So we should be interested in promoting the dignity and full spirituality that people gain through work. But this is not the issue in Jesus' command to give. God's desire that we work does not overrule Jesus' call for us to give. The Word is not to be pitted against itself.

BEING WILLING TO FIGHT

In giving, as in all of our doings, love should always be the rule. If we know someone who is asking us for money is on crack and in need of a fix, might love dictate that we withhold giving to them in that instance? Yes. Could the Holy Spirit give us particular conviction about how to deal with an individual who is begging from us? Sure. However, giving in some fashion should be the default setting for us, as Jesus teaches and demonstrates.

In the society of Jesus' day, drug addiction was not as great a problem as it is in our midst. We need to act with wisdom. But our hearts should be inclined toward generosity, and maintaining a generous heart will be a fight.

The world's influence on us is not neutral. It trains us not to love, not to be concerned for the well-being of another person unless we can benefit from it in some tangible or emotional way. We are taught to have little (if any) concern for people and to focus on ourselves—our reputation, our comfort, our desires.

Late on one bitterly cold night, I stopped my car at a traffic light next to a bus stop. A guy was waiting there, shivering in the cold. He was well dressed, wearing a coat that on a normal night would have kept him warm. We caught each other's eye, and he motioned a request that I give him a ride. I motioned back a denial. He then took out his wallet and fanned some cash toward me, indicating that he would pay for a ride. I shook my head again, the light turned green, and I pulled away.

I had responded by rote. You just don't pick up guys hitchhiking in the city, especially not in the middle of the night. It's dangerous. So on this occasion I did not think to ask God, to pray and seek the Spirit's counsel about what would be wise to do. I had not been trained well yet; I naturally went with the world's counsel. Many would say this was exactly what I should have done, for a hundred reasons. But sometimes when I have paused to ask God, I have felt led to pick up hitchhikers.

One late summer night, I was driving with Leah, a friend visiting from Alaska. We had been to a movie, and I was taking her home. We turned down a side street that was fairly dark, and a few blocks down my headlights illuminated a group of guys who were thrashing around together in the middle of the street. As the car got within about forty yards of them, they scattered, several on bikes and others on foot.

One guy broke out, running harder than the rest, in front of the car, as though he were running away from the others. As we pulled through and accelerated a bit, instead of running away from the car onto the sidewalk, he ran toward and alongside the car—on Leah's side. He was asking for help. I slowed down, and she cracked her window open to hear him better. He said he was being beaten and asked for help getting away from the guys who had scattered and were now some fifty yards behind us. I thought for a few seconds; Leah looked at me. And something inside me told me it was right to help this guy. So we let him in, and we drove him a mile or two and let him off where he said he would be safe.

It was a dangerous thing to do, no doubt about it. Who knows what he was involved in? And as we drove, he was not even beside me where I could see him; he was in the backseat. The world would deem my decision to help him stupid. But the people of the kingdom are to be a refuge to those in trouble and need. The Spirit counseled me to help him. And even if the decision had led to my injury (or Leah's), such results of acts of obedience are normal. Suffering for the sake of doing good is no strange thing. After all, was not just such a rescue operation performed generations ago at great cost to Jesus himself?

Then there was a guy who was hitchhiking on a bright spring day. He was dirty and poorly dressed, looking as if he might have slept on the streets more than a few consecutive nights. He looked healthy and certainly was in no trouble that I could see. But as I saw him from about a block away, the Spirit said to me, "Pick him up." So I did.

Surprised, he got in and said he was just going up the street a couple of miles. We talked for a minute about nothing in particular. Then he asked me if I was a Christian. I said yes, and he launched into about a ten-minute rant on the amazing nature of Jesus' life and his death—expressed in some of the basest cursing I have ever heard. Every third word was a different curse word, and all the rest were a familiar street jargon that people use to shoot the breeze with friends. He let me know how shocked he was at how Jesus lived, how terrible it was that his

Learning to Minister to the Homeless

Wisdom is certainly required if you are considering inviting someone into your home or ministering to them on the street. Many mental illnesses are episodic, and it is best to become acquainted with someone before deciding whether to invite them over. Addictions are a real and pernicious force in people's lives. If you hope to undertake ministry with folks in addiction, it is best to get some mentoring as you go, do it as a group and not as an individual, and be patient with your learning.

Elliot and Nathan decided to take an extended time—a two-year internship with Servant Partners—to explore ministry with the homeless. The jobs they took during this period got them involved. One worked for a nonprofit through a church; after a year, he switched to a public-sector job whose daily goal was to find housing for at least one homeless family. The other worked in the public sector helping people find the social services they needed. Their commitment also took them well beyond the work sphere. They invited some homeless men to stay with them for stretches of time, and they began to learn about addictions and mental illness from these men. They both learned a great deal about the poor, the law, the web of social services available and their city.

Along the way, as Nathan and Elliot took risks and were mentored, they also learned much about the Christian faith and serving the poor as an aspect of Christian spirituality. To be sure, they were taken advantage of. Some of their things were stolen. But that was not the most important thing to them. They persisted in love and did not allow their love to grow cold due to the evil of some. God met them in their faith journey and they are different men because of it.

Greg traveled to Pakistan to help those left in poverty by the great earthquake. Erna went to Tanzania to help those impoverished by the AIDS virus. Others have paid for a homeless family to have a place to stay for a month to get back on their feet. Some have started small neighborhood food pantries or helped people find jobs. There are so many ways we can choose to get involved, depending on our interests and convictions. What we choose to do may not be the central issue. The pertinent question is, "Will we choose to do something?"

friends deserted him and how awful and painful the crucifixion was. He shared how grateful he was and how unbelievable that God made this sacrifice for us.

We got to our destination and I pulled over. He said, "Thanks, brother," as he left. I think I laughed all the way home. I have never heard the life of Jesus recounted with more clarity or passion. I wish I had his rant on tape. Crass as it was, it was beautiful, in his own words, and captured much of what was important to him about who Jesus is. The gospel was indeed good news to him.

Now contrary to what you might think, I'm not all for picking up hitchhikers. These are the only people I have picked up and given a ride to in my life. It's not common. In fact, I don't often see people asking for rides these days. But my point is this: The kingdom of God is about being of service to others in a very practical way. It is about being concerned for the situation and condition of people who are struggling. Though it is a fight to continue to walk in this kind of love, members of the kingdom will display compassion to those in need.

These examples give a flavor of how the kingdom is opposed to the ways of the world. We must be trained by the Spirit of God to live and think in the style of the kingdom. Part of the good news of the kingdom to those in need is that God has not forgotten them and that in the kingdom their needs are just as important as the needs of those who have many material resources. Jesus' message is that they will not be overlooked or taken advantage of.

This is why James can say with such confidence, "Religion that is pure and undefiled before God and the Father is this: to visit orphans and widows in their affliction, and to keep oneself unstained from the world" (James 1:27). In the Bible orphans and widows, some of the most vulnerable people in ancient society, are representative of people in need. We are counseled to care for those in need who are vulnerable within our society. Further, we are shown that the kingdom and the world are opposed to one another. Actions and thinking in the world's way are implied to stain the believer. We see this again in 1 John 2:15: "If any one loves the world, love for the Father is not in him." And again in 3:17: "If any one has the world's goods and sees his brother in need, yet closes his heart against him, how does God's love abide in him?" This last passage seems to have as its context the community of faith, but it still bears the same message: if you are of the kingdom of God, care for those in need.

Should we help? If we ask this question of the Bible, its answer is clear: yes. And this answer applies when we just happen to run across a need or when we know of one that is outside of our immediate relational sphere—whether the person is a citizen or not, a resident of our country or of some other. Help for people in need is the command of the King, and it is a mark of his people everywhere. As we speak of God's kingdom, then, we give practical assistance as an expression of its reality.

We should exercise wisdom as we love, but the wisdom we need is largely gained through walking with God through life and not just through analysis or books. Practice in living out God's Word is the key. As we follow his Word and grow in sensitivity to his Spirit's leading, we will learn how to love more effectively. We should be eager to learn, not afraid of making mistakes, since the Lord will help us learn and always be there for us when in faith we make a wrong turn.

This can feel pretty risky at times. If certain things feel risky to you, consider that it might be a good risk of faith to step out and trust God by doing something you are not comfortable with.

SHOULD THE SYSTEM CHANGE?

> Is not this the fast that I choose:
> to loose the bonds of wickedness,
>   to undo the thongs of the yoke,
> to let the oppressed go free,
>   and to break every yoke? (Isaiah 58:6)

In many circles fasting is a forgotten spiritual discipline, left behind in a culture of gluttony. It is well worth our rediscovery if we desire to know the heart of God and see the power of God.

Back in the days of Isaiah, lots of people fasted. There were annual fasts, when everyone abstained from food together to seek God in solemnity. People also fasted in times of mourning, such as after the death of a family member or a close friend. Sometimes people fasted because of personal crisis or national emergency, when they needed God to come through for them.

At the time of the prophecy in Isaiah 58, God's people are in the habit of fasting. In a spiritual search for God's help and deliverance from their enemies, they abstain from eating. They seem to be asking God for righteous judgment against their foes—that he will make them victorious over the people with whom they are in conflict. As they fast, they are looking for God to answer them, to take note of their situation and to respond by crushing the enemies around them in the Middle East, making them victorious. However, in this passage, God's word to them takes a very different turn from what they expect. He does answer them, but listen to his words:

> Cry aloud, spare not,
>> lift up your voice like a trumpet;
> declare to my people their transgression,
>> to the house of Jacob their sins.
> Yet they seek me daily,
>> and delight to know my ways,
> as if they were a nation that did righteousness
>> and did not forsake the ordinance of their God;
> they ask of me righteous judgments,
>> they delight to draw near to God.
> "Why have we fasted, and thou seest it not?
>> Why have we humbled ourselves, and thou takest no knowledge
>>> of it?"
>
> Behold, in the day of your fast you seek your own pleasure,
>> and oppress all your workers.
> Behold, you fast only to quarrel and to fight
>> and to hit with wicked fist.
> Fasting like yours this day
>> will not make your voice to be heard on high.
> Is such the fast that I choose,
>> a day for a man to humble himself?
> Is it to bow down his head like a rush,
>> and to spread sackcloth and ashes under him?
> Will you call this a fast,
>> and a day acceptable to the LORD? (Isaiah 58:1-5)

You see, God's not playin' around, and he's not interested in religious ritual for its own sake. The Israelites felt so privileged with God. They felt so right about their lives and so entitled to what they wanted that they were blind to what their lives really looked like to God. He was less interested in how religious they looked; he wanted to see them actually living according to his word.

Well, that's too generous. Here's a better version. It makes God angry when people pretend to be serious about him but their lives reflect otherwise. When people go to church and sing up a storm and enjoy the preaching and go right back out and refuse health care to their workers and look the other way when someone is injured on the job, it invites God's wrath. He no more wants to hear all that singing than any normal person would want to stick their face in a pile of vomit. In the book of Amos he says,

> I hate, I despise your feasts,
>> and I take no delight in your solemn assemblies.
> Even though you offer me your burnt offerings and
>> cereal offerings,
>> I will not accept them,
> and the peace offerings of your fatted beasts
>> I will not look upon.
> Take away from me the noise of your songs;
>> to the melody of your harps I will not listen.
> But let justice roll down like waters,
>> and righteousness like an ever-flowing stream. (Amos 5:21-24)

To worship God in the midst of supporting injustice or benefiting from it does nothing more than disgust God and raise his ire. He hates and despises the gatherings of his people and their worship when they are not concerned with the things that really matter to him. Apart from substantive commitments to justice and righteousness, worship is a mockery of God. It may be good acting and look sincere, but God is not fooled by it. In his eyes it is bad acting. And apparently, in this instance, God doesn't like such actors. They tick him off.

The Isaiah passage goes on to explain that what really interests God is a fast from injustice, a fast from ignoring the plight of the poor. He is interested in our being of practical help to those in need and destroying the things that oppress people.

The yoke that is mentioned is an agricultural tool that harnesses the effort of oxen for plowing and other work. It binds them and directs them to the will of those who own them. God says he's interested in breaking or destroying the things that bind people in oppression. He wants to see people going free, being released from bondage. Later I will closely examine some structures and systems in our society that bind people in such a yoke. These are well-documented systems by which the poor are taken advantage of, treated unfairly and forced to do the will of those who (financially) own them.

Unfortunately, the people of God were not inclined to hear Isaiah's words. No revival sprang up in response to his preaching. The business community underwent no national repentance to set things right. They were not concerned with justice, the kingdom or the things of God; they were just concerned with themselves and getting what they wanted. Some might call it a spirit of greed or a delight in riches. Regardless, the prophet Habakkuk came along after Isaiah and had a clarifying word about this state of affairs. A paraphrase of the first few verses of Habakkuk 1 might read, "Though you cannot see it now, though the horizon may look clear, God is stirring up an enemy to do you harm because of your unjust and evil ways. Your refusal to repent will cost you and your nation dearly."

As you read on, I pray that you would ask God to help you be more concerned about him and his kingdom, more concerned about justice and righteousness, than about looking good, right and religious and getting the stuff you want when you want it. I encourage you to stop for a few minutes and pray about these things. Apart from the Spirit of God, the human heart has no more interest in the Word of God and the things of God than a pig has in pearls. We all need him to change us.

A JUST SYSTEM

Scripture does not stop at calling us to provide immediate relief for those in need. It also calls us to be agents by whom unjust systems and individuals are appropriately addressed.

The prophets speak to this in a corrective way, since they are teaching in times when things have gone wrong. However, in the books of the Law we can see God's intention that systems be set up which actually administer justice. For example, in Deuteronomy 15 and Leviticus 25 the Lord prescribes a sabbatical year and a year of jubilee that everyone in Israel was to observe. Every seventh year (sabbatical), slaves were to be released and all debts canceled. The people who were released from slavery were to be given something as they left. Scripture says that they must be provided for liberally from the possessions of the person they had worked for (Deuteronomy 15:12-15). Based on that principle, forty acres and a mule might seem reasonable. Every fiftieth year (jubilee), land that had been sold was to be returned to the person or family that originally owned it. People were to sell property accordingly, setting the price according to how close they were to the year of jubilee, when it would be returned.

In addition, the land was to rest: the people were not to farm during either the sabbatical year or the year of jubilee. God promised he would bring up a crop and that they would eat their fill without having to work the land. This system gave the people a structured break from work and business and a practical way to trust and see that it was really God who provided for them. It also provided a way out for people who were mired in debt, declared a year of amnesty for those who were so poor they had to sell themselves into debt slavery to survive, and redistributed to everyone a basic resource, invaluable in an agricultural (or any) society: land.

Together, the sabbatical year and the year of jubilee made up an amazing system that God set up for his people to live in. Even more beautiful, he gave them these instructions before they even occupied any land of their own. Scholars generally agree that there is no evidence that Israel ever practiced the jubilee as a nation. It seems they had a tough enough time observing the weekly sabbath and the sabbatical year. It may be that a spirit of greed rose up and persuaded them otherwise. For by the time of Jesus, they certainly seem to have been neglecting the substantive economic reforms of the sabbatical year. It is likely that those with power preferred to keep the advantages they had (through life circumstances, work or birth) over others. In our world such greed is not hard to imagine. But even if God's law was never fully practiced, it delineated a system that justly redistributed resources among people, though everyone did not have the same amount of wealth.

The discussion of the sabbath leads to an interesting reflection. Some of our economies and cultures actually are put together in such a way that the poor either struggle to get enough work or have no time to rest. A job that is fair allows the worker to rest a day a week. Rest would also imply sleep, since the way God initially structured life provided time for sleep and human beings were created to need to be refreshed in this way.

So the poor should have opportunity to work for a living wage—one that enables them to be self-supporting in their society—and should have opportunity for rest. How might a church create a means for the poor to rest in this way?

The Old Testament provides other simple systems of justice as well. Take the gleaning law. In Deuteronomy 24:19-22, God basically tells the owners of a farm field that at harvest time they must leave some of their crop behind for the poor. To get the food, the poor would have to come and pick it up from the ground or take it off the trees, but it was there for them. With a little work, they could have enough to eat. So in the Bible, it does not seem to be a problem to require that people do some work to gain food to survive.

Deuteronomy 23:24-25 allows people to eat freely from another person's field, though they cannot take anything away in a container or use a tool to harvest the crop. So anyone who is hungry can eat some grapes from a local vineyard, but no one is permitted to steal someone else's grapes to sell in the market. Through this command, the hungry are provided for and yet the owner's investment in the crop is protected. Maximizing profit for the owner of the field is not the highest value, nor is the protection of the field's profits for the exclusive use of that family.

In Deuteronomy 24:14-15, employers are told that they must pay hired persons their wage on the day they work so that their needs can be met. If they withhold the wage, it is sin. This protected day laborers from certain unjust financial practices of employers. The judicial system is to be free of bribes and of deference to the elite and moneyed of society (Deuteronomy 16:19). And when God's people are slack in these practices, God exhorts them to establish justice (see Amos 5:15).

These passages are examples of the legal code by which God sought to protect the lives of those in need and to be sure his people looked after each other. There were legal provisions to protect those with less wealth or less reputation or less of a voice in society. The rabbis, who interpreted God's law, considered giving to beggars a great and holy act. The legal, judicial, educational and health-care systems of our day are failing badly in providing for the poor and need reform.

THE CHURCH AND THE WORLD

A case may be made that such national or global reform is not the role of the church. Some Christians believe that since God gave the law and the prophets to his people (and not to other nations), the church should create its own economic system and institutions that are run on the basis of biblical principles. It would be a system within the overall system. This seems not only reasonable but central to the call of the church. We cannot simply work within the framework of the larger society and hope that reforms are implemented. We are called to live differently within the system of the world, and at times that will mean the creation of alternative communities, economies and institutions. The early church did not petition Rome to do a better job of caring for those in need; it created its own food pantry.

However, this impetus should not keep us from maintaining a loving concern for the world and participating in restraining evil, if not helping to bring reform. We can and should participate in local, national and global reform as we have opportunity, but there must be local, personal commitments that are of the quality that the Scriptures commend to us. A good principle is this: we should change the systems when we can, create new systems as needed, and accept the truth that all systems are fallen and will therefore be flawed.

3
COUNT THE COST

ONE DAY AS I WAS coming out of a church service, a very dirty, homeless-looking guy came up behind me as Jennifer and I walked toward our car. An older white guy with the look that long-term poverty and homelessness give to a man, he was pushing a shopping cart and walking slowly. I had seen him about a half-block away (when you live in the city long enough, you learn to be aware of who is around you on the street), but Jennifer heard him call out to us, while I had not.

So we stopped, and as is common in such situations, he talked to her, maybe thinking she was the softer touch, the easier mark. After listening to them and praying inwardly for a few minutes (and seeing that he was at least a little drunk) I entered the conversation and became the primary person he spoke with. He spoke with a slow Southern drawl and called me sir—a sure sign that he was from the deep South, as he claimed, and that his mother had raised him right, to be God-fearing. He must have been at least twenty years my elder.

Though looking for some practical help, he was eager to talk about church and the faith. So we talked for a while. He began to reminisce about the different churches he had been in and liked. "I like lots of churches," he said. "They are all great. I like Oriental church, Mexican church, white church, nigger church—they are all good. I've been to a lot."

Now let me just mention something to you: I am a black man. And when someone says *nigger*, it is not a neutral word. Maybe that's particularly true when a white man uses it, and maybe especially when it's an older white man speaking with a Southern drawl. It was loaded with all the historical baggage that it could have. He didn't use it as though he intended offense or even as though he were exactly referring to me. Maybe he was just being chronological. Jennifer is Asian, and sometimes I am mistaken for being Latino.

But I was taken aback a bit, being more familiar with the politically correct world of the linguistically challenged. I had to decide right then and there if I was going to allow what was clearly an insult to me and my folks (whether intended or not) to stop me from being of service to this man. He was the one who God had me run into on this day, and the question pressed me: *will I be a neighbor to him or not?* That was the real issue as Jesus put it in his story of the good Samaritan. Who would I be a neighbor to that day?

My dignity should be sturdy enough to withstand a little name calling. And though it has not always been so, God did help me to respond favorably to this man in the moment.

As I think back, I marvel at the things that were said and done to people who chose nevertheless to love. Jesus forgave people even as he hung in humiliation and excruciating pain on the cross. Martin Luther King Jr. chose not to lash out at those who said and did terrible things.

I could have said a variety of things to the man. But, in the moment, I would have said them out of a desire to correct his language, to have him speak to me more respectfully or to embarrass him, not because I loved him. Correction isn't always a bad idea; sometimes that kind of conversation is needed. But in this instance my fiancée and I needed to be bigger than an outdated derogatory ethnic term.

NOT NEW NEWS

The teaching of Jesus is not really new. Rather it is old—a revisiting of God's commands in the Old Testament. He simply lived out and taught the ways of the kingdom in his era. That too is our task. And since the Scripture is full of commands to care for those in need, what might that old news look like in a new situation? Isaiah 58 tells us that the Lord wants us to share our bread with the hungry, bring the homeless poor into our homes, share our clothing with those who need some and not hide ourselves from the rest of humanity. How might we work this one out?

On one cold night, Bill met a beggar. They stood talking outside a restaurant, and both men were cold. The beggar shivered, wearing only a thin shirt. The guy was not literally naked, but in the cold of that night he might as well have been. Without being asked, Bill took his shirt off and offered it to the man.

Richard, Ellen, Tim and Caroline picked a drunken man up out of the gutter and cared for him until he was better. I know people who have taken hungry beggars to lunch and sat down with them to share a meal, taking the opportunity to get to know them and sometimes to pray for them.

Then there was the kindness that Reid, Dave and John showed to Robert. While in college these young men developed a friendship with Robert, who was struggling on the streets. One night they invited him to join them for dinner and treated him to a meal at the school cafeteria. Then they invited him to stay over in their room that night after their Bible study. He agreed.

Before long, word had gotten around the dorm that there was a homeless man on the floor. The resident assistant heard and called security, and three of the largest security guards we had ever seen showed up in the hall. They were so big that two of them could not walk side by side as they went down the hall. They proceeded, along with the RA, to ask the guys about the incident. The conversation went something like this:

"Is there a homeless man in the dorm here? We heard that there was."

"Our friend Robert is here. Is there a problem? We are allowed to have friends in the dorm, aren't we?"

Silence, awkwardness and an eventual departure ensued. Dave, Reid and John washed Robert's clothes and offered him the chance to take a shower. By the end of Robert's stay, they knew what it was to be hated by the world. But they also had a witness to what the kingdom was about like few others, and people either hated or loved them for it, depending on their perspective.

COUNTING THE COST

I once knew a man named Ron who was homeless and in need of help. He would come by and work for a few dollars in the yard of the house I was renting. Over the course of several months, life on the streets (and a drug habit) began to take its toll on him. He wouldn't go to a treatment center for help but couldn't seem to get straight by himself either.

One morning, as I was rushing to get ready to go to a meeting, Ron showed up at my door, cold and soaking wet. It was raining hard, and he had been caught out in it. I needed to shower and get dressed in a hurry, but I told him to come in and sit by the heater while his coat dried out. As he sat there, I offered him something to eat.

As I hurried to fix breakfast for him, I thought, *Now no one else is home. We have a general policy that we don't leave people we help alone in our house. I need to take a shower. Should I have him leave?* I decided I would be quick in the bathroom. I put the breakfast down in front of Ron and hurriedly took a shower. I took, at most, five minutes in the bathroom. When I came out, there was an empty plate, an empty chair and an empty space where my bicycle used to be. The front door was wide open. Ron was gone, and I haven't seen him since.

Here was a guy I, and others I lived with, had regularly helped, say twenty times or so over the past six months. Ron knew that I, and others I lived with, would help him if he needed it. And yet in the midst of receiving help, he chose to violate that trust and steal my bicycle. Not only so but, unknown to us, he had unlocked the window next to where he had been sitting—and he came back that night and stole another bike.

To say the least, I was pretty steamed. I went looking for him that morning, but after a few minutes I let it go and went on to my meeting. Such was the cost of love that day. Still, I didn't like it, and I wrestled with the situation. I didn't like being taken advantage of; my trust had been violated; I felt stupid. It bothered me that I had lost my bike and that my friend had lost his. Honestly, for a little while I cared more about finding Ron and the bike (I looked for it as I drove around the next couple of days) than I did about him as a person.

Not that we should want our stuff stolen. It's wrong. It is a violation of trust, and such things do hurt. Sin injures us. But Jesus is very clear about these types of things. In Luke 6:30 he says, "Of him who takes away your goods do not ask them again." Now here is a word that may cause much of humanity to choke. It is best not read while one is eating or drinking. It goes down sideways that when someone—an enemy acting unjustly—takes our things, we should not seek the restoration of those goods. In our highly legalized society where everyone sues everyone for everything, this is scandalous.

I am not suggesting that there is no place in the kingdom for the redress of grievances and the execution of justice in criminal cases. There are other biblical passages to explore. However, Luke 6:30 does provide this command that goes in direct opposition to the spirit of law and the flurry of lawsuits that engulf the courts in the United States—and such activity between believers is as common as among those of the world. Jesus doesn't say people have to be grateful or even treat us well when we help them. His directive is to love others, even enemies. Such love will cost people of the kingdom something. It cost Jesus his life.

Sometimes love may come at great cost. There have been some who have suffered greatly by being people of kindness—Scripture tells us that this will be so. The parable of the sower tells us that there will be suffering that comes on account of the word of God in us. Paul, counseling his young charge Timothy, says that "all who desire to live a godly life in Christ Jesus will be persecuted" (2 Timothy 3:12). Jesus tells us that we should not be shocked when we find that the world hates us, because it hated him first (John 15:18).

It should be no surprise that these things happen. We should expect it, and we should expect to be mocked by the world—called foolish and derided for being dimwitted. People think that a life spent pouring out costly love is a waste. In truth, it is a beautiful thing. In Jesus' own day, many thought that his life of love and service, culminating in the crucifixion, was a waste. But there was no more beautiful life ever lived. For what is despised in the world is honored in the kingdom.

Jesus' death, his crucifixion, is not only the means of salvation, it is also the method. It is the path for all disciples, and as we work for justice this certainly becomes apparent. "Whoever loses his life for [Jesus'] sake and the gospel's will save it" (Mark 8:35).

IT'S WORTH IT

Love is worth the cost. We never know how God will use our concrete love to do a beautiful work in a person's life. In fact, the life that is changed may very well be our own.

One summer I took a few weeks to help some third- and fourth-graders get some needed academic help. They were far behind in their schoolwork. I had about a dozen of them for about six weeks in a public school that loaned space to us over the summer. Each of these kids was behind in school. Each of them lived in the area and came from a family that was struggling to make it. Throughout the summer I helped them learn to read, spell, do math and write. We played on the playground with other kids and their teachers. I visited their homes and met their families. I prayed for them and sometimes with them and their families. Two of the boys came from a local boys' home. They were struggling the most and needed the most attention in class. It was clear that these kids needed my love and presence. They needed the love and presence of God through our time together that summer.

But they weren't the only ones benefiting from our time together. With those children I felt as though I had found something of the kingdom of God. I found my voice and leadership to a degree not previously known. My vision for God's work and sense of his presence became sharper. My awareness of God's love stretched: each person on the street, each child, each family, each beggar—each one is someone for whom the Lord gave his life. I learned about the ways families struggle and the way the educational system works. Though an outsider, from the middle class and well educated, I felt at home. God changed my life as I met him among those children that summer. It was a turning point in my life, one I will never forget.

On another occasion I went to harvest corn and cucumbers in the heat of the summer in Virginia with a group called the Gleaners. They were older men and women who went out to harvest the crops of fields that were about to be plowed under. The government was paying a farmer to plow under certain fields in order to keep the price of crops at a given level for all farmers. Limiting the supply in this way, as long as there is steady demand, stabilizes the price farmers get for their crops. Of course it also happens to waste food that could be used elsewhere, if not in the United States. Under Old Testament laws such fields would have been made accessible to the poor, who could go and get something to eat if they needed it. But today, many poor people live in urban areas and have no access to the fields, even if they were allowed to pick. That was why this farmer had made arrangements for the Gleaners to come.

I rode with the Gleaners early one morning from Washington, D.C., to harvest part of the farmer's field. We worked for a long time through the heat of the day. It was my first time harvesting, and it was no easy work. Corn husks cut into your hands—not as badly as cotton does, but it's bad enough.

We piled up a bunch of corn and then went over to pick cucumbers. We got more than the Gleaners were accustomed to, since there were a few young hands this day. In fact we loaded so much food into the vans that one of them blew out a tire on the trip back. We delivered the food to a food pantry run by the Sojourners community.

It was a very creative way to care for the community and work with some of the people who would receive help from the pantry. The richest part of the experience may have been hearing the Gleaners' stories as we worked together.

Loving the poor has cost me something. There were weekends and whole summers when I could have done other things. The work took time. Sometimes it was inconvenient. Sometimes—like when a four-teen-year-old in our youth group was shot and killed—there was heart-ache. Some people I've worked with had to deal with their family's harsh criticism. Resources could have been spent in other ways. But I and those whose stories I have told have no regrets; it was entirely worth it.

A few years back I knew a guy who worked at the corner gas station. He would pump your gas for you and clean your windows for change. He wanted to work for what he was given. (Interesting that not long ago these services were provided by gas stations that employed people to serve their customers, before the days of self-service.) When asked, he called himself Red, and he could be found at the station most days of the week. Two of us got to know him a bit over about a year, and we were glad to pay him to clean the windows on our car. But then he suddenly stopped showing up at the station, and I never saw him again.

After some time my friend ran into someone who knew Red and found out that he had begun working a regular job, had found faith in God and was now a deacon in a church in another city. We were glad that God let us see some of the fruit of our love for him, small though it had been, over the months. What an amazing thing. We could rejoice with others, people we didn't even know, about God's redemption of Red, while people who had walked by him and ignored him could not. We had been given the opportunity to invest in the work of God in him. And such investments had sustained him and had been used by God, along with many other more significant investments, to minister to him and redeem his life. As we had talked with him, we did not know what God was doing. We had just a bit part in this story, not a starring role, and we had to trust that God would make use of the love we gave, even if we never saw the fruit of it. Who would have thought that God would use our small acts of kindness to help Red on his way?

All of us need to ask ourselves: Do we see the value of each person this greatly—as Jesus sees them? Are we willing to love them, even in the smallest and most practical of ways, or will we run on with our business and preoccupation—with our list of things to do, distracted by concerns that are ours and not really God's? Are we willing to have the bit role and not be the star?

These days, I'm just glad to be in God's play at all. I hope to be able to do small acts with great love. Let us give ourselves in hope that in the economy of the kingdom, no act of love is wasted. And let us pray that our hearts beat with God's concerns and our eyes see things his way. God may use even the smallest service of people in need for their redemption.

I hope some day to hear good news about Ron.

4

GIVING A MAN A FISH

GIVE A MAN A FISH and you feed him for a day.

Teach a man to fish and you feed him for a lifetime.

The next three chapters divide up the discussion of what some call justice ministry into three categories that I hope will be useful. The first category is direct relief or, as the slogan says, giving a man (or woman) a fish. Direct relief can be thought of as directly giving resources to those who need them. Food, clothing and shelter are basic needs that must be addressed. This work can be personal and relational in nature or carried out through organizational efforts. Maybe it is best when we have some personal involvement and some larger organizational commitments as well. The combination gives us a broad perspective and helps keep our hearts connected to what is happening.

The second category is the provision of skills. Chapter five will explore the means by which the cycle of poverty may be broken at the individual or familial level through the provision of a level of skill that permits employment options. Sometimes poverty is cross-generational, with families having been poor for as long as anyone can remember. Although we may provide these families or individuals with direct relief, it is equally important to help people gain the means to become self-sustaining. Work is important, and we need to have the practice of teaching others to fish, even if we do help them with something to eat today.

Third, we will look at addressing systemic injustice that exploits the poor and even encourages poverty. Such systems may be entirely intentional, created to do what they accomplish—hold the poor in place while some other group takes advantage of them and benefits monetarily. Examples from earlier times are the apartheid system of South Africa and the system of slavery in the United States. However, in other systems the disadvantage to the poor may be incidental—circumstances and independent decisions that combine to have an oppressive effect. In either situation, the people of God have a responsibility to address these systems. At times this will mean reform; at times it will mean prophetic protest. At other times it will mean the creation of a whole new system as a way to deal with the problems. In any of these cases, the believing community is working on behalf of (and, in the best cases, *with*) those in need.

Scripture clearly makes a place for direct relief efforts. Such efforts may use at least two different means: personal involvement and directing resources through an organization. In either instance, we are given the opportunity to help those in need when immediate assistance is necessary. The most direct scriptural command about direct relief that I have found is Jesus' one-liner "Give to every one who begs" (Luke 6:30). That's pretty clear. The old adage about teaching a person to fish is fine. But if she is hungry today, we are instructed to share what we have right now. Then we may attend to teaching her how to fish and work alongside her to deal with any obstacles that might prevent her from fishing effectively.

PERSONAL INVOLVEMENT

A number of passages, like those discussed earlier, call us to have some direct involvement in relating with the poor. This could involve any of various kinds of interactions. It could mean talking with a beggar or visiting an elderly shut-in. It could mean offering work to a day laborer and maybe choosing to work alongside him. It could mean offering health care to the family of migrant farm workers. It could mean helping pick up a beaten or drunken man in the gutter.

Richard, Tim, Caroline and Ellen moved into a poorer part of Los Angeles because of their conviction about these things. One day they found a man sleeping in the gutter outside the house they were renting. Though it was a busy street and many cars were driving by, no one had thought to help him up or care for him. No one had even checked on him. For all they knew, he could have been dead.

So the four did what any kingdom person would do: they went and checked on him. Finding him alive but not well, they brought him into their home. He rested there and later took a shower and had something to eat. After staying a day or two, he was better and went on his way.

The Gospel of Luke records a similar story in chapter 10. Sometimes we just need to do what Scripture says in a literal way. But even if we did not have the good Samaritan parable, if we were in the same position, would we not want to be checked on and helped? We know how we would want to be loved, and so we should offer the same. This kind of living, according to Jesus, is the sum of the law and the prophets (Matthew 7:12).

During their first year in the neighborhood, this team of friends also met a man named Clarence. Clarence was a veteran, and, possibly due to his war experiences, at times he had difficulty remembering accurately and talking coherently. He was a large, barrel-chested man and a very kind soul.

One day Clarence showed up at my door looking for Richard, with whom I was renting an apartment. He seemed troubled. I introduced myself, and we talked on the front steps for a while. Clarence did not look well, but as I found over time, this was not uncommon. He was generally a bit dirty, and he was also incontinent. His pants were regularly stained with urine marks, and the smell drew flies.

Richard showed up. As we considered whether to invite Clarence to stay over, God reminded me that my father had served in the Korean War. I was challenged by the thought, *What would I want someone to do, if this were my dad?* The answer was pretty obvious.

We had a meal together, washed his clothes, put out a mattress with a blanket and made it easy for him to get to the bathroom in the night. We left the bathroom light on, cracked the door open and put the mattress about ten feet away from the bathroom door. Then we all went to sleep in our respective rooms.

I woke up in the morning, came out to check on Clarence and found out that I had slept through quite a ruckus. Clarence had woken up in the middle of the night, needing to go to the bathroom. Knowing he had only a moment, he rushed to get up, and instead of grabbing the doorknob to the well-lit bathroom, he grabbed the knob to Richard's bedroom door. He threw it open with some force and rushed inside. Richard awoke to the noise and, half-awake, saw the silhouetted image of a large, agitated man in his doorway. Startled, he jumped up on top of his bed, ready to do battle. Clarence was just as surprised to see Richard, and he went—right there in the doorway.

I had slept through all this mayhem on the other side of the apartment. By the time I got up, these were all semi-comical memories and the urine had been cleaned up. We laugh about it now, but in the moment it wasn't so funny. Sometimes love is a little messy.

Cori met a woman who regularly begged outside the gates of the university where she was a student. Several other students got to know Linda; I also met her, and we developed a friendship over about eight years. Linda was the best actor I have ever known or seen—including those on the big screen. She could turn on the tears instantly if she thought it would compel you to give her some money. She could lie with convincing authenticity about her need for clothes and then go and sell them to support her drug habit. As Cori reflected, "There were a lot of things I learned from being with her. One thing I learned was not to give a homeless person a duffle bag full of clothes. The next day I ran into her, and she was so high she didn't recognize me—and she asked me for clothes again."

But when you called her out on it all, Linda would snap to, admit her game and then just talk with you. She had a place to stay but was indeed poor and at times in poor health.

Cori took a special liking to Linda. She felt drawn to minister to her, to befriend her and love her. And over time Cori found true the words of Jesus in Matthew 25: as she ministered to Linda, somehow she encountered the Lord himself. Simply by being with her, Linda taught Cori more about who Cori was, who God was and what it meant to be part of his kingdom. It was a personal seminary class, you might say.

Over Cori's four years in school, she had an ongoing friendship with Linda. They would pray together, and sometimes Cori would help her with a ride or a meal. Linda became someone to her—not just a statistic or an annoyance or an inconvenience, but a person.

Now it happened that after Cori graduated and began to work, God did something unusual. He continued to run her into Linda at odd times. So, partly by intention and partly by divine appointment, the relationship kept going.

Through some years, Cori watched Linda grow thinner. Sometimes she looked better than others, but overall she was weakening physically. Then for a while they lost touch. Cori prayed and asked God that if Linda was dying or had died, he would somehow let her know.

One day, Cori received a phone call from her friend Fina, a nurse at a local hospital. Fina was working a rotation in the emergency unit, and a woman had been brought in. The paramedics had found her unconscious on the street. No one knew who she was, and there was no family that they could find. Fina came into the room to be of help, looked at the woman's face and recognized her. It was Linda. She thought Cori might know Linda's last name so that they might be able to find some family members. Cori did know Linda's full name, because some years earlier Linda had signed a birthday card for her.

Cori went to the hospital, and they tried to find and notify any family members. No one was found. So Cori visited with Linda, prayed for her and spent time with her as she died. Cori had a deep sense of God's love for Linda and wanted Linda to know how much she was loved. Linda never regained consciousness, but through Cori, her family was with her as she died.

How beautiful of God to honor the relationship he had given Cori and Linda. Though they had lost touch, he appointed one last meeting: a time for Cori to love Linda again, a time for Linda to be cared for personally in her final hours, a time for the humanity and dignity of two sisters to be affirmed, a time to say goodbye.

Ideas for Getting Started

1. If someone is begging for money for food, take them out to eat or prepare a meal for them. Eat with them and talk with them. Offer to pray with them for their circumstances and tell them a little about your own needs.

2. Volunteer some time at a food pantry or serve a meal at a homeless shelter.

3. Visit a convalescent home that houses residents who are economically struggling; talk with the people about their lives and share about yours. Offer to pray for them or with them.

4. Maybe you don't live in a very urban area, but many smaller cities have pockets of poverty—sometimes in trailer parks. How can you get to know people who live in places like this and learn about their lives and needs?

Ask God for ways to personally get involved. You never know where God might lead you. My friend Mark followed the call of God to minister on a Native American reservation. It is out in the middle of nowhere. Like the people around him, he lives in a home with no running water and no electricity. Though Mark's concern for the poor did not lead him to the city, it has led him to a highly relational expression of incarnational ministry among the poor.

We should be committed to personally assisting those in need. The relationships themselves are of infinite value. What riches, what beauty and love lie in store for us if we will follow the Lord in his ways. Though it is a way of suffering, a way of hardships, it is the way of knowing him and his love for us all.

Direct relief of another's suffering is a high form of love. Sometimes it requires our money; frequently it requires our time. But most of all, it requires that we see the value and dignity of each person we interact with. It requires that we see who they were created to be more than who they are. It requires that people be more important to us than the list of things we have to do that day or our possessions. It is, after all, the people around us who are eternal, not the stuff we use or the money we make.

THE WITNESS OF COMPASSION

One of the beautiful things about this kind of ministry is that talking about God seems to come so naturally from it. One Japanese student who was in the United States on an exchange program came with us to a central park one day for a time of sharing food with those who were hungry and praying for them. He could not believe his eyes. First of all, he had never seen anything like this before. He could not help but ask why we were doing it. It seemed so right to him, but so foreign. The chance to talk about God and the gospel was right there. Sometimes our good works lead to good witness.

Two friends of mine were homeless two years ago and were sleeping in a park. We started our adult fellowship meeting on Sunday mornings there in the community center. After the service, we would serve a light lunch, and we would invite those who were sleeping in the park to come and join us for a meal. These two friends got food at the end of our church service for weeks and then left immediately. Only after a while did they stick around long enough for members of our church to get to know them. The gift of the food built a bridge of trust that just walking up to them in the park and trying to talk with them about Jesus couldn't have. One of our members helped them get into temporary housing. After a while, they began to join us for worship. About a year ago, they were baptized. We do need to add words to our works, but practical love can open up to opportunity to relate about the gospel by demonstrating it.

As you may know, there are literally millions of squatters around the world who live in makeshift housing on land that they do not own in and around large cities. This is some of the result of the urbanization of poverty. These people's homes may be destroyed by the government of their nation with virtually no notice. They have no legal rights to the land and can lose everything in a moment. Often there is no electricity or running water. Many of these people do not know Christ, and there is little witness among them worldwide. By the estimates of one missionary, if grouped together, they could be considered the largest unreached people group in the world.

It is well worth considering whether as believers in developed countries we should partner with indigenous believers in these nations to see churches established among these squatters that are concerned with evangelism and electricity, communion and community transformation, healing and health care, righteousness and land rights. Some mission agencies are doing just that; I have listed some in the appendix.

DIRECTING RESOURCES

The other way to be involved in direct relief is through giving money and other resources through reputable organizations. In these opportunities there is not much relational opportunity. Thus to avoid patronizing and to actually understand what is needful and loving to give, I believe we should have actual relationships, at least periodically, with some people who are in need. But in concert with this, we may contribute to organizations that build those personal relationships and serve a wider need in the community. Whether they work in another country or are involved locally, these are organizations, institutions and nonprofit groups that offer assistance.

Our money goes an especially long way toward helping people in very poor areas overseas. The cost of living is not as high, and a little of our money can make a significant difference in the life of a family. Sometimes assistance given to one or a couple of family members can sustain a whole family and break the cycle of poverty.

Let's say a group of four college grads take this seriously and decide to live together simply for a few years and give generously to ministry efforts. Let's say they all are engineers and get entry-level jobs at fifty thousand dollars a year. They rent an apartment together in a less expensive neighborhood and live on a relatively meager budget. Even with taxes and the need to pay back student loans and such, these four could give roughly eighty thousand a year to support ministries that are making an impact. This amount is figured for an area where the cost of living is one of the highest in the United States. Even if these four maintained the arrangement for only a couple of years, they would still have plenty of time to invest, save and make prudent long-term decisions. It would just mean delaying or derailing certain things like a costly condo purchase.

There are many responsible ministries around the world to which one could give; I will offer some well-known and some less prominent examples. The Adom Project is a ministry of a local church in Ghana that hosts a school. It was begun by a pastor who visited the United States for a time to go to seminary, working his way through school as a janitor at a Presbyterian church. The school was gradually built and there is hope for another building. The children are provided with a meal and some basic health care on site. There are opportunities to sponsor a child, to help build the next building and for small groups to visit for short stretches. Compassion International also offers opportunities to help children in various countries with basic health and educational needs, while also giving them opportunities to learn about Jesus. Food for the Hungry offers similar assistance.

Opportunities in the United States include agencies such as the

Southwest Community Center in Santa Ana, California, which provides food and clothing for families in need. The Catholic Worker (in various locations) has a wonderful local ministry for homeless people; various sites serve meals, provide some shelter and are significantly involved in advocacy for the poor. In Philadelphia, the Enterprise Center offers training in business skills to troubled youth. Spirit and Truth Fellowship in Philadelphia and Rock Church and Lawndale Community Church in the Chicago area offer many opportunities to minister to those in need. These are some of the ministries that I am familiar with in different parts of the country. But you should look for what God is doing around you and be willing to explore. Some ministries in the Christian Community Development Association may be of help to you.

1. If you choose to become involved with an organization, do some prayer, thinking and research about what kind of work you want to contribute to. Then choose to be involved for a few years. For example, if you choose to sponsor a child with Compassion International or the Adom Project, it would be best if you chose to stick with that child for several years in order to stabilize their experience and that of their family.

2. Know the organization you give to. Financial accountability is important, and you should know how your money and resources are being used and have good evidence that this is actually happening. There are some scams out there.

3. If you would like contact information for any of the ministries mentioned here or others, please consult the appendix.

5

TEACHING A MAN TO FISH

DISTRIBUTING SKILLS

MY WIFE AND I SPENT SOME TIME in the slums of Bangkok, Thailand, with some other missionaries, helping them navigate team dynamics as they worked to plant two churches. A woman named Nihm became a Christian and began to minister in the slum areas. With the help of the mission team, she began to offer assistance to other squatters in two areas. One area of focus quickly became the development of a savings cooperative in which families could save together to purchase property. They knew that a new highway was scheduled to be built and would run right through their part of the city. Their homes, though poor, would be demolished—it was only a matter of time.

Savings in general was unheard of in the slums, but doing it together and depositing it in a bank for a long-term goal like this was ridiculous. Yet as Nihm told people her own story and some of the pain of her life, they too began to open up about their lives. She then talked with them about where she went with her pain. She told them about Christ and his power to strengthen and heal. And she taught them how to save and work together.

By now sixty families have joined and are saving toward purchasing a plot of land. They are now working with a government program that

may offer them a very good loan. Some have found faith in this journey; they have been drawn to God through the good words and works
of Nihm. And through God's work they have been given the practical
skills they needed to see their lives change.

THE MINISTRY OF EMPOWERMENT

Though in many situations we do need to give a man (or woman) a fish,
the proverb is still true—giving alone is not enough. We should help
them to learn to fish for themselves and be self-sustaining, able to make
a living. It is a helpful thing to give bread to the hungry and clothing to
those who find themselves unprepared for the winter. Going further,
some Scripture passages encourage us to give people who are hungry the
opportunity to work for food. The gleaning laws mentioned in chapter
two are examples. The next step in real service to those in need is to offer
any type of skill or insight to help them be self-sustaining.

There is great wisdom to having people work. Scripture tells us that
work is actually part of the created order of things, not part of the Fall.
Work became more difficult for humanity due to sin, but the truth of the
matter is that we are made to work in the world. Now though this is true,
it does not mean that our value as human beings is to be tied to our work,
our ability to work or how much we produce by our work. Such notions
are cultural and have nothing to do with the kingdom. But that being
said, we have a great need to actually be engaged in work of some type.

People who have spent time with men and women without jobs or re-
sponsibilities know how debilitating this can be. Our sense of purpose
and our spiritual health are partly tied to working. If a person has been
without work for an extended period, their sense of dignity and their
countenance rises when they begin working. Some have not worked for
so long that evil spiritual habits become the norm, and then, as sin de-
ceives them, they are convinced that working is actually worse for them
than receiving a handout. Handouts are needed. But to contribute to a
person's humanity, dignity and kingdom purpose, we should labor to
help them gain the skills necessary for self-sustaining employment.

In Old and New Testament times trade skills were passed down family lines. People generally learned from their families how to be a carpenter or fisherman. Education was very practical in this sense. Those with the greatest vested interest—parents and other family members—trained those they cared most about. In our system today, someone who may not even be from my neighborhood trains my child in skills that are only very distantly related to most professions that the child has any clear sense about or interest in. As adults we can see the value of the skills for later in their lives, but the kids cannot see this clearly. There is no immediate connection or payoff for them, and in our culture of immediate gratification this is a big problem.

The investment of many teachers in the education of our children is admirable. My mother taught for forty-three years in the public school system and devoted herself to the children in her classroom. By the time they left her class, they had picked up some things and were ready to move on. Some teachers are simply overwhelmed by the numbers and problems in their classrooms and cannot do what they would want to do. And as in any profession, there are plenty of teachers who teach simply because it is a job that they do for a paycheck. Maybe they didn't start in that place; maybe they got worn out and disillusioned along the way. But if a child gives them trouble or isn't really learning, they do not have the motivation of a loving parent who recognizes the problems and responds with the loving personal attention, rewards and discipline to get Johnny to learn.

One teacher told a friend of mine that his son would never be a reader. The kid was in the middle of elementary school. Today, several years later, he loves to read and is well beyond his peers as he makes his way through middle school.

Unfortunately, though, most children who are caught in these situations through no fault of their own grow up without the means to gain adequate employment. Research shows that children who fall behind early in school tend to drop out eventually. This not only encourages delinquency and criminal activity but also limits the jobs that they will have access to as adults. Children cannot see this or do anything about the school systems, teachers and other adults who are failing to provide them with the skills they need. And there are immense predatory forces that seek their lives. I will come back to this topic later; for now, suffice it to say that there are spiritual, social forces, forces of evil and death, that seek to shape the hearts, minds and lives of these children, and these forces are concentrated with great power against them. Thus we must address the spiritual roots of poverty and oppression as well as offer some skills that may help until a better system can be put in place. Children can be helped to learn through tutoring programs and mentoring relationships that will supplement their school experience.

Providing skills is a very important middle step in thinking about and working on justice issues, for it stands between direct assistance and systemic change. We should labor to equip people with the skills they need to be self-supporting in the society they live in. And though the reason for the lack of skills may be in large part systemic, it is still appropriate to address these needs at the microsystem level. In effect, by ministering on a local level, we augment the current system or create our own. This is how the early church generally operated when true institutional reform was not an available route. The first Christians did not reform government programs to feed the poor; the Roman Empire did not allow for reform, so the early church created its own system to feed the hungry. This approach does not address the larger system, but it is a step in that direction, and it is a prophetic witness to the world.

EXAMPLES OF THESE MINISTRIES

Distributing skills can be done in a variety of ways. Some agencies provide training in a trade for little or no charge. People can learn to be plumbers, electricians, mechanics or skilled practitioners of other trades if they apply themselves. These are jobs that make good money and are regularly in demand. They could provide steady income for a family.

Rachael, a senior in college, works in a tutoring program that is addressing the lack of grade-level reading skills among elementary-school students. Though it is an enrichment program, it is very skill-centered and encourages a love for reading.

Fina, a nurse by trade, spent time with neighbors who didn't understand how to negotiate the health care system and helped them understand the choices and decisions they needed to make. She helped them navigate the current system knowledgeably—necessary if one is going to get results.

Derek brought some neighborhood boys over to help him put a wood floor in his house. They enjoyed the work, the time together and learning from him. It took awhile to finish the floors (probably longer than if Derek didn't have the boys), but they were all glad they came. The boys now have some understanding of what carpentry is like as well as a sense of accomplishment.

Ellen gets together with a friend or two to help them learn English. To participate in the larger life of the United States, to help their kids negotiate the school system and to interact effectively with systems beyond it, this is a very useful skill to have. The gatherings are social and fluid but appreciated by all. And Ellen gets a chance to practice her Spanish in the process.

Others help people learn how to deal with loans and buying a house. Some help teach house upkeep or financial management. There are so many ways training can be provided for those in need that it is simply astonishing.

Of course a key in all this is for no person to relate in a demeaning way to any other person. The challenge for people with resources and education is to not look down on those who have less. Human though this is, it is not godly. Rather, partnerships should be established with both people on the same footing. Both recognize that they bring something to the partnership, if only in themselves. As we strive to think about things in this way and establishing a means of self-sustaining work, we avoid creating a dependent relationship. People are creative and don't always need others to solve their problems for them. When they participate in solving it, or when they solve it by themselves, they are the stronger and wiser for it.

This said, we must recognize that some people will not be able to be self-supporting. Due to illness, age or injury, some people will need our financial and material support for the long haul. This is not a problem but an opportunity for people to continue serving one another. There can still be partnership, love and mutuality, even when the money flows only one way. Henri Nouwen's reflections on ministering to and learning from the mentally handicapped would be a good read for anyone wanting to explore more.

PREVENTIVE MINISTRY: VISION FOR THE FUTURE

In general, it is far better to be engaged in training work with people at an earlier age than a later one. Ministry to children and youth is *preventive*. It prevents their delinquency; it prevents their criminality; it prevents their incarceration. It promotes their competency, their employability, their dignity and ultimately their citizenship. Those who are engaged in these ministries understand this. It is far easier to help children and youth get what they need than to provide skills to an adult who has learned to not learn, has engaged in criminal activity, has been incarcerated because of finding no meaningful way to be involved in society, and has been effectively denied the ability to acquire a reasonable standard of living and preserve their dignity. It is far easier to preserve and nurture a child's dignity than it is to repair an adult's—though with God all things are indeed possible.

Desiring both prevention and neighborhood transformation, Kim and Chris, newly married, moved into a mixed-income neighborhood in order to participate in starting a ministry there. In response to God's call, they rented an apartment on a residential street that was particularly known for gang activity, drug and alcohol abuse, and prostitution. They lived across the street from me.

One evening they showed up at my door looking nervous and a bit shaken. They had come home from work and found their front door ajar. They briefly opened it to find their apartment in disarray. They came over to our place and called the police. No one was there; the burglars had gone—but their wedding gifts had departed as well.

They felt very violated by all this, and as we talked and prayed together over the next couple of weeks, they struggled with whether they should stay in the neighborhood. Chris felt particularly concerned for the safety of his wife. Those of us who had moved into the neighborhood always knew that such a burglary could happen, and we had talked about it ahead of time, but now it had actually happened to someone—that is always different.

A few days later, Kim was talking with her next-door neighbor, and she mentioned that many things had been stolen from them. Rosa was indignant about it. She felt it was particularly insulting for someone to do that to newlyweds. Soon Rosa showed up at Kim's door with a covered can on wheels. She had packed a few extra things that Rosa's family decided to give to the Hawleys. Through their conversations over the next few days, Kim got to know more of Rosa's family, and a friendship developed with one younger daughter, Esther. Esther was struggling in school and was not very motivated to do better. But she did like spending time cooking with Kim.

So Kim made a deal with Esther. She would help Esther learn to bake various pastries, but Esther would have to learn to read the recipe instructions. In a very short time this developed into a small business, and of course we all bought cookies. Through this experience, two things happened for Esther. Her reading improved significantly, and she became a very good student. Her grades soared, and she was pretty motivated. And she also found God in the process and decided to become a Christian.

Though difficult, Chris and Kim's willingness to suffer with other neighbors who were also frequent victims of the local burglary racket gave them great opportunity to serve and witness. This event, and their decision to stay, was used by God and broke open a network of relationships with adults in the neighborhood. Esther got the skills she needed and found Jesus along the way. It was a beautiful example of the costs and power of an incarnational witness.

A STRATEGIC MINISTRY

We must offer skills to the children, youth and adults who desire them. They should not be overlooked. For even if we desire systemic change, this will take time, and compassion would dictate that those who need help now receive it as we work toward changing the system.

If we have any vision, we will appreciate and support meaningful work with children and youth. This is a godly priority. But also, as some advocates have pointed out, it is wise fiscal policy. There is a clear correlation: kids who do poorly in school and drop out are more likely to end up in prison. It costs a great deal to keep people in prison. The prison industry is an issue in itself, but my point here is that it is far less costly to educate young people through college (and possibly even to employ them at a livable wage). Mark Twain is quoted as having said, "Every time you stop a school, you will have to build a jail. What you gain at one end you lose at the other. It's like feeding a dog on his own tail. It won't fatten the dog." We have to spend money if we lock people up. Would it not be wiser to choose to spend that money in advance and gradually decrease the total prison population?

Of course some would consider this questionable fiscal policy. But a society that effectively refuses a substantial portion of its population any real way of surviving with a reasonable standard of living, yet declares that it is about "liberty and justice for all," is self-contradictory. Then to declare that those who have been denied access to the system's benefits are ruining our society and must therefore be removed, and to imprison them after three strikes as though this were a baseball game, compounds the error. The prison system treats them with contempt and subjects them to abuse, and instead of providing genuine opportunities for rehabilitation and redemption allows them to be beaten, raped and killed. This is scandalous.

I realize that there are some very hardened people in prison, some very violent, dangerous men and women. Many belong right where they are and need to be there a very long time. But what about giving them opportunities for redemption while they are there?

Remember the apostle Paul: as Saul, he had been responsible for the persecution and deaths of many people. Lots of people would probably have cheered life in prison or a death sentence for him. But God ministered to him, and his life was changed. He became a greater force for good than he ever had been for evil. I hope for such stories of redemption for others.

There are some great things about our country, but our imprisonment and recidivism rates are shameful. The number of mentally ill people in prison (and their treatment) is also disturbing. Yet the resources that we have, the relative calm and the possibilities for economic gain are tremendous, especially in comparison to conditions in many other nations. The judicial and prison systems in Malawi, for example, are ugly. Some inmates live in cells where there is barely room for them to lie down next to one another. Some stay there for years because their case papers have been lost. Our problems are significant, but we need to maintain a global perspective. We should be interested in efforts to establish God's justice not only locally and nationally but internationally as well. We must choose to be part of the solution and not part of the problem. We must engage meaningfully in justice work to provide needed skills to children, youth and adults.

If we have any interest in the well-being of our country, we will apply ourselves here. The United States' fragile gang prevention programs, the lost national war on drugs, the overloaded judicial system and the overcrowding of the prison system may all be addressed in part through effective "teach a man to fish" programs. Who knows, these problems may be coming to a neighborhood near you. Rather than put bars on our windows, buy a car alarm and a gun, let's get together, do the work that needs to be done and pray that the Lord will bless our labors.

6
FIXING THE POND
DEALING WITH THE SYSTEM

SOMETIMES WE CAN HELP deal with an immediate crisis for an individual or group of people, and we can provide the skills necessary to improve their situation in the long run and gain a means of support, but there are other factors that can prevent them from becoming successful and self-supporting.

To return to the fishing analogy: We may feed someone with some fish that we caught and offer our pole to teach him how to catch a fish. He may use our lures and bait and even fish in our favorite spot for a while. We may help him become savvy to particular times to fish and learn certain tactics that will help him succeed. Then, after we have provided relief, after he has gained needed skills, we send him on his way. He heads home only to discover that the cost of a fishing pole is too high for him, the store in town won't sell him one anyway (they don't sell to his kind), the local fishermen have overfished the lake that's a mile away, and the river near his house is polluted.

If we are to actually deal with the root causes of poverty, some of our work will have to be done at the systemic or environmental level. To be sure, some people are poor due to their own sin. We really don't need any help becoming poor and coming up against serious problems; given our sin, all of us are quite capable of messing up our lives. Personal sin must be addressed in justice ministry, as in all ministry. But our efforts simply must not stop there. In truth, some people are poor due to the sin of others, or due to local or national disasters, or as a result of the effects of generational sin, either in their family or in their community and nation, or simply due to family crisis.

My wife and I just had a son. He spent a couple of days in intensive care due to a slight temperature. The tab—$49,000. And this is for a pretty healthy kid with no substantial birthing complications. If I hadn't had health insurance, I would currently be trying to find a way out of serious debt.

We fall short of really honoring the Lord's desire if we only throw some money, food and shelter to the homeless and do not address the causes of hunger and homelessness—especially if they are structural in nature and not simply the results of drought and famine or personal sin. Scripture calls believers to be directly involved in these issues, and we should pray against unjust systems as well. Jesus' commentary and actions in the temple's court of the Gentiles are a fine example (Mark 11), as is the exhortation of the prophet Isaiah to break every yoke (Isaiah 58). Amos also cries out for justice to be established in the judicial system of his day.

Given that the Scripture exhorts us to address systemic problems, why do we have such difficulty doing it? There are plenty of roadblocks. Consider the following parable.

There once was a place on the highway where many accidents occurred. The leaders of a local church became concerned with the suffering of the people who had been hit by cars and those who had been injured in collisions. So they took up a collection and improved the local emergency care response time. They even got an emergency phone line installed at the intersection so that accident victims or witnesses could get in touch with the authorities quickly if no cell phone was available. They also increased the capacity of the local hospital emergency room.

Then someone proposed, "Why don't we get the highway reengineered so that it's not so dangerous?" So they began to lobby the city council to add a lane, create better visibility and widen the dangerous curve. But it was discovered that a prominent businessman in the congregation had his business near the crucial spot on the highway, and his company would be adversely affected by the proposed changes. The church leaders thought about this and laid down a decision: Any further political action to change the highway would be unwise. The gospel is (the thinking goes) not political, and there is to be a separation of church and state issues. The congregation dropped the issue but continued to care for those who were injured and for the families of those killed on the highway.

Even with clear teaching in Scripture, there are personal, social, relational and political reasons that we don't want to get involved with changing systems. But these things are best addressed rather than avoided. In the case above, the highway needs to be altered and church members should stay involved to ensure that it happens, but they should also be concerned about their brother's business. Could he be helped so that he doesn't have to unfairly shoulder so much of the burden of the highway reconstruction? Seems to me that something could be worked out. We can learn how to deal with conflict, to talk in a civil and respectful tone, to look out for each other and to love sacrificially. That's a tall order, but it is the path that mature believers should walk.

Now before we go on, please stop and pray and ask God to help you hear this in the right way. Some of these topics taken up in the remainder of this chapter are very ugly, and I pray that you are neither discouraged nor soured by the discussion. We need to face these harsh realities head on. We need to see them clearly with God in the picture, whose very presence changes situations and possibilities. But at the end of the chapter you will read a hopeful story—the story of a man who engaged with unjust systems and helped to bring change.

SYSTEMIC FAILURES: POOR PLANNING, CORRUPT DECISIONS

Have you ever thought of planning as a ministry? If people planned well and developed low-income housing, severe housing shortages would not exist in our urban centers. There are water usage and waste concerns in our cities. Though some local, state and federal guidelines for the use of grant money explicitly state that new developments must include a certain percentage of low-income housing, I know of one city that deliberately refused to build such units. Its leaders did not want those kind of people in their city. A friend was in on the meetings and personally protested these arrangements, but her voice went unheard. Those in charge reasoned that the places were already being built and they would be satisfied to pay the fine that officials imposed. They did so and moved on. They paid the penalties, and the poor still went without needed housing. The monies that should have helped were misused, and someone is getting rich from the project. Believers can bring such abuses to the attention of the public and people of power. Sometimes a little light on a situation creates enough heat for things to change.

Another municipality was given funds to expand a park area. Open public space was desperately needed in this area. In many of our major urban areas, open space is very limited and population density is too great. Greater population density is a significant factor in the increase of violence. But in this case, though many residents wanted the park expanded, city officials refused, saying that they did not want to expand the park because they knew what would happen: "All the Latino families from adjacent areas would come and camp out on the weekends."

Other cities, seeking to renovate the inner urban core, decide to remove their services for the poor. They offer to buy ministry properties on the basis of the greater city interest. They offer the possibility of giving these ministries places in some other part of the city. In one case, curiously, when they were turned down, inspections from the local fire marshal began. Or zoning ordinances are changed to move the organizations. Various pressures are brought to bear.

It works a little differently in each situation, but the story is largely the same. Pressures and issues that had come up periodically but always had been resolved in a way amenable to all parties now escalate as facilities are shuttered. In one case, housing was demolished to open space for new low-income units, but with only half the living capacity. All the residents were "temporarily" relocated while the demolition and construction were carried out. Just where are half of the residents supposed to go after the work is completed?

Well-crafted plans, if exercised with some foresight, could have made a great contribution to the well-being of many families with meager incomes and little voice in public policy. They were not in the board meetings, as were some of my friends who watched, heard, objected and were ignored. Those in power in these situations failed us all. When possible, we should hold such people to account and rectify the wrongs. As Zacchaeus understood, sometimes repentance means reparations (Luke 19:1-10).

SYSTEMIC FAILURES: PUBLIC SCHOOLS

Jonathan Kozol has eloquently documented some of the failures and injustices of the educational system in the United States. He reveals people marked by cold indifference, casual ignorance and, among those who have money and other privileges, outright defensiveness and hostility. There are many well-meaning people in the school system, but there are many who obviously don't really care at all or understand even the basics of what is happening. I commend Kozol's works to you for your own research. The stories he tells are even more compelling than the statistics.

Kozol sees the basic funding inequity in public education in the United States as a systemic problem:

> The number of teachers over 60 years of age in the Chicago system is twice that of the teachers under 30. The salary scale, too low to keep exciting, youthful teachers in the system, leads the city to rely on low-paid subs, who represent more than a quarter of Chicago's teaching force.

The answer is found, at least in part, in the arcane machinery by which we finance public education. Most schools in the United

States depend for their initial funding on a tax on local property. There are also state and federal funding sources, and we will discuss them later, but the property tax is the decisive force in shaping inequality. The property tax depends, of course, upon the taxable value of one's home and that of local industries. A typical wealthy suburb in which homes are often worth more than $400,000 draws upon a larger tax base in proportion to its student population than a city occupied by thousands of poor people. Typically, in the United States, very poor communities place high priority on education, and they often tax themselves at higher rates than do the very affluent communities. But, even if they tax themselves at several times the rate of an extremely wealthy district, they are likely to end up with far less money for each child in their schools.

Because the property tax is counted as a tax deduction by the federal government, home-owners in a wealthy suburb get back a substantial portion of the money that they spend to fund their children's schools—effectively, a federal subsidy for an unequal education. Home-owners in poor districts get this subsidy as well, but because their total tax is less, the subsidy is less. The mortgage interest that home-owners pay is also treated as a tax deduction—in effect, a second federal subsidy. These subsidies, as I have termed them, are considerably larger than most people understand. In 1984, for instance, property-tax deductions granted by the federal government were $9 billion. An additional $23 billion in mortgage-interest deductions were provided to home-owners: a total of some $32 billion. Federal grants to local schools, in contrast, totaled only $7 billion, and only part of this was earmarked for low-income districts. Federal policy, in this respect, increases the existing gulf between the richest and the poorest schools.

All of these disparities are also heightened, in the case of larger cities like Chicago, by the disproportionate number of entirely tax-free institutions—colleges and hospitals and art museums, for instance—that are sited in such cities. In some cities, according to

Jonathan Wilson, former chairman of the Council of Urban Boards of Education, 30 percent or more of the potential tax base is exempt from taxes, compared to as little as 3 percent in the adjacent suburbs. Suburbanites, of course, enjoy the use of these nonprofit, tax-free institutions; and, in the case of private colleges and universities, they are far *more* likely to enjoy their use than are the residents of inner cities.

Cities like Chicago face the added problem that an overly large portion of their limited tax revenues must be diverted to meet nonschool costs that wealthy suburbs do not face, or only on a far more modest scale. (*Savage Inequalities,* pp. 54-56)

Police and fire department costs and public health expenditures are among those he lists as competing with education in the budgets of large cities.

The fundamental question that arises is, why are we so committed as a nation to the education of some of our children and not others? But other issues also are of concern. How is it that we have employed teachers who are doing nothing for the children they are entrusted to instruct? How can kids learn in a classroom that is very cold or regularly has sewage overflow in it? How can some children have no books and some teachers no supplies with which to instruct? How can we have shootings and muggings and virtually riotous conditions on some high school campuses and not be up in arms about it? And how can we expect one person to instruct thirty, even under optimal conditions?

The practical answers are a little involved; the history takes some study to understand. But the gist of the matter is this: there is a well-educated, well-financed, politically involved group of people in the United States who are not motivated to do anything about the terrible disparities in our schools. In response to the shame of and public outrage over a particular crisis, they (we) may act to alleviate the problem—but often the solution is only temporary.

I understand that this is a harsh and sweeping claim. Feel free to test it with your own research if you like. But the bottom line of it is this: some children—the most vulnerable group of any society—don't get even a remotely fair shake at learning. We haven't provided them with a level playing field—and the glaring gaps in opportunity are not merited.

Throughout the United States, these trends are heavily slanted against people of lower incomes and darker skin tones. This system needs change. It is unjust. And there is great resistance to a fundamental reformation of it.

Let's say there is a failing school system and people are caught in a generational poverty cycle. What if we did educational reform at the systemic level? Let's say we shifted the funding some, reduced class sizes, made good educational material available to everyone and required teachers to perform at a substantial level of competency. What if while this was happening we encouraged skills ministries to continue and made a significant push for volunteers who really cared about the education of kids and youth? Maybe we could throw in some extracurricular investment—afternoon and weekend activities. If done at the same time, within fifteen years, maybe less, there would be a substantial benefit to the poorest of communities as well as a likely reduction in the incarceration rate of people from these communities.

Some people, in response, are actually trying to walk in pursuit of justice. Some of these are distributing skills. People are laboring to help kids who are not getting what they need. They are running or staffing educational and enrichment ministries. Some try to help out through big brother–big sister types of mentoring. Others seek to provide direct relief. They raise funds from the business sector to help with particular school projects. Some donate books for the school library. Some parents even come in to serve as teaching assistants at no cost.

These are outstanding responses to a clearly unjust situation. And though they leave the weight of the inequities on the backs of a few, that is frequently the way systemic injustices get addressed. But should we not change the system that is creating the inequities, struggles and problems?

If a patient needs a heart transplant, shouldn't we take her in for surgery rather than just offering aspirin, pain medication, dietary restrictions and an exercise regimen? This is a critical condition, not on the level of hiccups or the common cold. The broken system itself needs to be repaired or replaced, not just helped along.

Am I overstating the seriousness of the problem? Not in the eyes of those who attend a failing school and must endure these hardships. And not to those who see with good-Samaritan eyes. Not to those who would inherit eternal life.

SYSTEMIC FAILURES: BUSINESS PRACTICES

The historical banking practice of redlining is another example of an unjust system. In case you are not familiar with this practice: Some banks routinely refused to invest funds—loan money—to people in certain neighborhoods. Residents of these areas could not acquire home loans or business loans, because the banks viewed them as a bad risk. The practice is called redlining because, as best as I can figure, bank managers would draw a red line around certain neighborhoods on the city map and would not cross that line to make loans. Not surprisingly, one reason was the perceptions of certain kinds of people— that lower-income people or members of certain ethnic groups were bad risks. Of course this was a somewhat ironic position to take as an institution, since the banks were more than willing to receive the money of people in these communities and make a profit by investing it elsewhere. But they refused to offer any real benefit to the people from whom they were profiting handsomely.

The practice of redlining was altered by legislation that forced banks to make loans in these neighborhoods. Banks now have to reinvest a portion of their loans in the communities from which they take their deposits. How this is monitored and what system of accountability there is I do not know. But people who lived this history and know the current loan scene tell me that things are better. Still, sometimes unjust policies are decided behind closed doors.

Redlining parallels a complaint the African American community has had against certain stores in their neighborhoods owned by other ethnic groups: there is no reinvestment, only a taking of resources from the community. Rarely is any of the money that customers pay for the store's products used to employ people from the neighborhood, or invested in a community project, or spent on other goods and services that come from local black-owned neighborhood businesses. Businesses need to make a profit, but what profit margin and at whose cost are valid questions.

It has been a joy to see and hear of some store owners who have taken steps to address these issues on their own initiative, without being forced to do so by legislation or community action. And it has been a joy to hear of some residents discussing the problems in civil terms with a store owner, instead of resorting to hostile action. There is a need for more mediators and bridge people in these situations.

A Latina friend of mine, Lisa, grew up in an urban area that was mainly Latino and Anglo. As she became a teenager, the city began to gain some significant Asian presence. Just as she reached the age to begin driving, her parents' insurance rates rose precipitously. Lisa was not yet driving, so she wasn't the cause of the increase. Her mother called the insurance agency and asked several agents why the rates had gone up so steeply. At first she was told that they were increasing in general, city-wide. In a later conversation, it came out that the company was increasing rates in their particular section of the city.

Finally Lisa's mother talked to someone who either didn't know to keep his mouth shut or didn't agree with what he saw happening. He confided, "Well, the rates are increasing because your section of the city is becoming more Chinese. The Chinese population is growing rapidly."

At hearing this she was puzzled, so she asked a reasonable question. "What does that have to do with the rate hike?"

The agent responded very frankly, "Well, due to the slant of their eyes, Chinese people have poor peripheral vision. They are a greater risk to insure because they are more apt to get into accidents."

You may need a minute to recuperate from this story—if so, take a deep breath, fuss and laugh about it for a minute, and then come join the discussion again.

Funny, over the years I've played basketball with a bunch of different Asian guys with slanted eyes. These guards seem to have great peripheral vision, frequently better than that of folks I've played with of other ethnic groups. This is only my impression, of course—not a scientific study, a survey, the findings of a clinical trial or anything of the sort.

The insurance agent's comment reflected an impression—also not the result of a scientific study. It was an insider comment offered as though this were common knowledge that would be readily accepted. After all, "we all know that blacks are less intelligent than whites. They should be slaves." Or the more modern version: "They can't be quarterbacks, much less head coaches." Or an equally flawed though greatly heralded version: "You know all white people are racist"—as though it were genetic. Even if clinical studies had been done with Asians to prove that they have poor peripheral vision, to justify higher insurance rates it would be necessary to prove that this actually results in more accidents or more serious accidents over time. It would also have to be proved that this was the specific variable among many that led to poor judgment or response time.

On a personal note, having lived for many years now in a city with a significant Asian population, I must acknowledge that I have seen far more serious accidents among drivers of other ethnic groups. Maybe we should lower Asians' insurance rates. Just an impression.

SYSTEMIC FAILURES: OTHER FORMS OF DISCRIMINATION

Some of us can't believe that this kind of thing still happens. But it does.

It has been proven, for example, that it is more difficult for a black man to get a cab in New York City than for a white man, even if they are dressed the same and hail the cab in a similar way.

An African American friend of mine, needing to use the restroom while walking through a business district, was turned away by a bank employee, who said, "We don't have any bathrooms available for the public."

Just as a test, an Anglo friend who was accompanying her waited a while, then entered the bank and asked the same employee about a restroom. She was welcomed and shown the way to the restroom.

I'll let you guess what ethnic group the employee belonged to. Let's just say that she wasn't black.

Didn't we solve all this business about segregated bathrooms, lunch counters, drinking fountains and theaters a few decades ago? I guess not. But who would have known if my other friend had not had the sense to test the system's integrity and the integrity of that employee? It seems that these issues of race and class are still around.

Our judicial system's favoring of wealth and people of lighter hues is well documented. Bacre Ndiaye, a Senegalese lawyer and death-penalty expert serving with the United Nations, completed a study of the application of the death penalty in the United States. In a 1998 report to the United Nations, he concluded, "The imposition of death sentences in the United States seems to continue to be marked by arbitrariness. Race, ethnic origin and economic status appear to be key determinants of who will and who will not receive a sentence of death."

Along the same lines, an article published by the *San Francisco Chronicle* on April 26, 2000, reported that "African American and Latino youths are treated more severely than white teenagers charged with comparable crimes at every step of the juvenile justice system, according to a comprehensive report released . . . by the Justice Department and six of the nation's leading foundations." Several examples are offered. The article summarizes the facts thus: "For young people charged with a violent crime who have not been in juvenile prison previously, black teenagers are nine times more likely than whites to be sentenced to juvenile prison. For those charged with drug offenses, black youths are 48 times more likely than whites to be sentenced to juvenile prison." The length of incarceration varies greatly between these two groups as well. An article in the *Los Angeles Times* says the evidence is overwhelming: "Pulling together the most comprehensive data yet on race and crime in America, two recent reports show that, at every stage of the nation's system of crime and punishment—from arrest through plea bargaining to sentencing—black and brown Americans get tougher treatment than whites" (May 22, 2000).

Certain laws, such as those that impose harsher penalties for possession of crack cocaine than for possession of the powder version, should be reconsidered and revised. But our laws are not the principal problem. Many of the justice system's inequities are the responsibility of the judges and juries that decide cases and participate in sentencing. Let's face it, whether he did it or not, if O. J. Simpson were poor, he would be on death row. Or take the case of Winona Ryder, who was caught shoplifting on videotape at a very high-end Beverly Hills store. The evidence was unassailable, yet the prosecutor went into the courtroom seeking no jail time for the erring celebrity. Let's just say that this probably wouldn't have happened if it had been a different kind of person in the store or if the theft had happened in a different part of town.

Plenty of other issues also merit our attention. Whose backyards do dumps get placed in and freeways run through? The environmental exploitation of poorer communities is a grave injustice. Offering people a living wage is critical. We could look at the costs of fair housing for both rental and home ownership in many areas. The practice of double-talk in regard to immigration must cease. We cannot prosecute and persecute illegal immigrants and still build an economy on their cheap labor. The shipping of manufacturing jobs abroad has eliminated opportunities of employment for many U.S. residents and has sometimes encouraged exploitation of the workers of other countries. Health care availability for the poor is another whole arena.

There are plenty of issues, plenty of opportunities to work for justice, plenty of work to go around. We can't all do everything. The concerns are many, but we need not be overwhelmed by them. Rather, we should simply recognize that everyone cannot do everything but we should all be involved in addressing injustice. We should pray and partner with those around us as we work to build a more just nation and neighborhood. Until the kingdom of God comes in fullness, we will always have the opportunity. The poor will always be among us.

CHANGING THE SYSTEM: A STORY OF HOPE

In 1954, Walter Schoendorf moved his family to San Jose, California, after he accepted a job as a plant manager for the Safeway Corporation. The son of German immigrants, he had grown up in Jersey City, not speaking English until he entered elementary school.

The Safeway job was his first managerial position, and he began at the candy plant. There he had many Mexican employees, and one day agents of the Immigration and Naturalization Service showed up unannounced. When nearly half of Schoendorf's workforce took off out the back door, he was shocked. He was also angry: he had hired many of the men through the unemployment board in the area, so he thought they were legal. He was also angry that the INS would show up unannounced.

When he talked with his foreman, he was told that the workers were simply uncomfortable with the INS and afraid of being mistreated. They were scared. So in response, he decided to get any who did not have legal status enrolled in the guest worker program of the time. This allowed them to stay for up to six years and work at the plant without being harassed. Then as they worked, he arranged to have them trained in higher-level skills. This meant that when their guest-worker status ended, they could apply to reenter the United States with a good possibility of gaining legal immigrant status.

Even while they participated in the guest-worker program, Schoendorf paid them more than ten dollars an hour. In the 1950s that was a competitive working middle-class wage, and they had full benefits. Further, while most companies forced their employees to use their two-week vacation every year, Schoendorf allowed his workers to accrue up to five weeks so that they could visit family in Mexico.

Thus one man engaged a system for the betterment of those he worked with. Moreover, he provided skills training that benefited the workers and helped them get established long term. But the story doesn't end there.

In 1967, Safeway began building a new plant in Richmond, California. Schoendorf was good friends with Bishop John Cummings, head of the Oakland Diocese of the Catholic Church. The two men had discussed the extensive unemployment within the African American community. Schoendorf agreed to target the African American community to deal with what seemed a system of employment that excluded many of its members. Working with Catholic Social Services in Richmond, he created a mentorship program for African American men in the community. African American supervisors already at the plant began to mentor these local men in all the skills needed to run the plant. About 85-90 percent of the men who went through the program became lifetime employees of Safeway. The program provided skills and helped to transform part of the system of employment. Walter Schoendorf's business practices thus led to community and family transformation.

As a person of faith, Schoendorf believed using his power and authority to help others was the right thing to do. Today, he and his grandson Mike are often surprised and saddened to see examples of business practices that were clearly not crafted with the benefit of employees in mind.

For larger-scale examples of system changing by citizens of other countries, you may want to research South Africa's process of transformation in throwing off the system of apartheid, or the largely nonviolent revolution that deposed the Marcos regime in the Philippines. A resource providing the testimony of one person who was involved at the ground level of system change in the Philippines is listed in the appendix.

Microlending programs can address certain structural inequities at the local level in many countries. Offering small loans with training in financial management and helping people create a workable business plan has worked well in many places. Some ministries have found microenterprise effective in helping to generate more sustainable economic development.

Finding and helping community leaders to engage their own problems is an important related strategy. Secular groups frequently call this community organizing, but the Bible describes a very similar process in Nehemiah. Usually the best thing is not to solve problems for people. As a general rule, their participation is central. Some leaders feel strongly that we should never do for people what they can do for themselves. This helps curb dependency and can facilitate genuine partnership.

SYSTEMIC FAILURES: FOREIGN POLICY

If you are an American, what I am about to tell you may be hard to believe and more than a little controversial. It is not controversial because it is debatable. The facts have been verified. But it is controversial because what most of us have been taught about our country is only a portion of the truth and has been taught from the vantage point of our national economic interest. In a fallen world, it is the winners who get to write the history books, excluding some distasteful facts and spinning others to put them in the best light.

The United States has used political, economic and military force to undermine social movements and economies in a whole host of countries. Much of this was kept from the eyes and ears of the American public but has been revealed through various whistle-blowers within the government. The tales are ugly ones of sending funds, training military commanders in torture tactics and providing weapons for the murder of millions of people—all with the fundamental motivation of preserving U.S. economic advantage in the world.

In *What Uncle Sam Really Wants,* Noam Chomsky lays out this dynamic in the most practical of terms. He quotes a policy document written in 1948 by George Kennan, who was in charge of long-range planning with the State Department:

> We have about 50% of the world's wealth, but only 6.3% of its population. . . . In this situation, we cannot fail to be the object of envy and resentment. Our real task in the coming period is to devise a pattern of relationships which will permit us to maintain this position of disparity. . . . To do so, we will have to dispense with all sentimentality and day-dreaming; and our attention will have to be concentrated everywhere on our immediate national objectives. . . . We should cease to talk about vague and . . . unreal objectives such as human rights, the raising of living standards, and democratization. The day is not far off when we are going to have to deal with straight power concepts. The less we are then hampered by idealistic slogans, the better.

In Chomsky's words, "To pacify the public, it was necessary to trumpet the 'idealistic slogans' (as is still being done constantly), but here planners were talking to one another."

This book, as well as other works listed in the appendix, provides a careful record of U.S. actions overseas that have served the poor very little and frequently done them great harm in order to gain economic advantages for the United States. It was not really all about democracy, or even capitalism. Here is a quick set of examples from Chomsky:

> Parliamentary governments were barred or overthrown, with US support and sometimes direct intervention, in Iran in 1953, in Guatemala in 1954 (and 1963), in the Dominican Republic in 1963 and 1965, in Brazil in 1964, in Chile in 1973, and often elsewhere. Our policies have been very much the same in El Salvador and in many other places across the globe.

Meddling in the affairs—including democratic decisions—of other countries has been justified on political and economic grounds, but it has been argued most forcefully for the purpose of national security. Though such actions are difficult to justify on any biblical grounds, usually before long moral rationalizations begin to be offered. While humanitarian reasons for many covert and overt military actions have been cited, they have been a smoke screen for other motives. All of this has come at great cost to the poor of the world.

Though space does not permit exploring these issues in depth here, they merit examination by anyone in the United States who knows the Lord. As noted, the appendix lists a few short resources that will help begin your journey. As you read and learn, keep a few principles in mind:

- A war of information is being waged constantly.
- Propaganda is not fact.
- There are people with vested interests and a lot at stake.

You do well to ask plenty of questions about the information you get and the sources you receive it from.

During many U.S. interventions abroad, the American public has been kept largely ignorant. Today, Internet technology gives us access as never before to international news and investigations—but it has also given rise to a logjam of reporting. Sifting through this is a job for whole groups of people, not solitary individuals.

Nations must, by nature, respond to military threat and attack. Of course lies and misleading information do not help anyone make an informed decision about what is right to do. Since we live in a democracy (though some would argue with this view) and democracies of our kind are built on an informed and educated citizenry, we must hold leaders accountable when they generate misleading information that prejudices our decisions. Intentional lying in such a situation seems a grievous sin. Yet, as others have found, Democrats and Republicans have lied to us.

Please do not take my statements as manifestations of anti-Americanism. Nor do I intend to promote democratic or republican agendas. I do not mean to advocate for capitalism or any other economic theory either. I am just saying, let's take the Bible seriously and be about the whole gospel. If we let the values and teachings of Scripture be the plumb line, we see how crooked things really are.

Each of us will likely have more direct involvement in one particular part of justice work. There is still a need for more classic missionaries, but there is also a need for educators, business managers, administrators, doctors and many other professionals to serve ministries of justice. There are plenty of jobs to go around, and if we work together, if we pray, if we plan and if we persevere, we may, in the Lord, accomplish good for many people.

We need to take care along the way, lest we lose our way and forget who we are following, what we are after and why. But we should move forward and address these things as we go. Let's not just create another think tank and sit on the issues. Instead, let's thoughtfully act and reflect and learn with those around us, happy to have the Lord direct us as we minister, much as he did the disciples.

These are immense problems, and their gravity should grieve us. Seeing the society of his day, Jesus wept. In our own society, like the leaders of Jerusalem, we frequently do not know the things that make for peace. Our tasks may range from prayer to prophetic presence, but in all of this we should be hopeful, knowing that God is at work in our world. In the midst of it all, the kingdom is yet coming.

If we engage what is going on in the world, we must accept that things will be messy and there will be great suffering. But though we fully engage this world, our hope does not rest upon it.

7

RACE AND CLASS

AMONG SOME OF US, the term *race* is not popular these days. In truth, race—the concept common in the United States—is not a scientific term. It is rather a created sociological concept that at times serves only to further divisions, making us think we are more different than we in fact are. In-depth genetic studies have affirmed this in recent years.

Yet though we know that the concept has little scientific basis and it may have been used to divide us in the past, it persists within the conversation on the street. The guy on the street still thinks of and uses *race* to refer to people who look (and sometimes act) a certain way. So though the war of words to get rid of this concept is worthwhile, it is still important to speak in terms people understand—to teach, as it were, from where they are.

The truest distinctions lie not in appearance but in how our appearance affects the quality of life we enjoy. This quality is due in part to the experiences we are subject to due to our appearance. There are important differences among people groups that are cultural and related to social class—differences in how people think, act and see the world. But mostly due to the idolatry of appearance (read race) in the United States, our appearance has a great deal to do with the kind of life experience we have. There is such a thing as racism, even though there is scientifically no basis for the idea of race as we know it.

I make this point because due to our history, race and class are intertwined in the United States. And because this is so, issues of justice in this country invariably include currents of race and class. It's true in other countries as well, of course. The fact that black Africans were forcibly brought here and enslaved and the fact that today there is a substantial black underclass are not unrelated to each other. Slaves were emancipated just before my grandfather's oldest brother was born. That is three generations. Only two generations separate me from the actual institution of slavery in the United States.

The fact that many Latino children are in the poorest schools and the worst neighborhoods and have some of the worst dealings with our police and judicial system is not unrelated to the fact that at various points in our history, people of a lighter hue decided that their generally darker brethren were to be thought of differently and closed down the opportunities that they once enjoyed.

The experiences of Asians have varied depending on where they came from and how they got to the United States. Some in the Asian community came to this country with substantial resources. Others came as refugees.

Many authors have done the research and connected the dots regarding the experiences of minority ethnic groups. I shall not labor to reproduce their work here; if you are fuzzy on this issue, or if you don't believe me, investigate for yourself. In the appendix I have included some recommended readings. Some of them are long and detailed, but they represent well the history that is not usually taught in school, except in specialized college courses.

But for this discussion, what needs to be said is that changing structures and promoting reconciliation are intimately related. And so we must not simply address the system and the powers that be. Our only focus, or even our central focus, must not be legislation or adjudication. We must not stop with integration and appropriate representation of certain ethnic groups in certain places. We must move toward relational reconciliation, a making of peace and the expression of heartfelt sacrificial love across race and class lines.

The work to alter social structures will not change things on the deepest level. They may make things slightly better here and there. But if someone hates you, even for a false or unjust reason, there will still be strife. And if they have the power to do so, they will find a way to take advantage of you. Such is the human heart and condition. We must not simply address power. And yet we must address it.

THE DEBATE

For many years now, people who seek justice and healing have engaged in a debate about whether a relational approach or a power-based approach is most effective in addressing class and ethnic disparities. The relational camp reminds us that we are called to be the family of Christ. Various reconciliation passages in Scripture focus on broken trust between individuals and the need for forgiveness. Relational advocates, then, claim that the gospel calls us to relate to one another in regular, authentic ways. These high-trust, redeemed, integral relationships will provide a solution-from-within for injustices within society. The idea is that better relationships will result in greater compassion, truth, equity, justice, and ultimately, peace in our society. Sometimes the approach of this relational group is very emotional or very conciliatory.

The power-based group seeks up-front commitments for power sharing between dominant and underrepresented or oppressed groups. Sometimes this conversation leans toward reparations and the need for immediate decisive action. It is on the basis of such actions that relationship can begin or be restored. Sometimes this approach is advocated graciously, other times with a rather aggressive and confrontational style. A popular slogan is "No justice, no peace."

There are gradations within each approach, but many people or groups fall solidly on one side of this fence or the other. But the fence seems to me a useless divide, like so many other divisions among believers today. The church should be about being family across ethnic and class lines. All should be welcome, and as believers we should be marked by forgiveness and authentic love for one another. The church should be about resolving substantive power issues in economic terms, in decision making, and in civic inequities within the believing community and in the world. We should have a corrective prophetic voice and presence in our society where that is necessary. The Scripture offers all of this. There is no separation in the Bible, and there should be no separation among us. All of this is part of our birthright and our marching orders as believers.

Warm, fuzzy feelings between people are of such fleeting presence that after they have passed one might wonder if they were ever genuine. They are only ghostly shadows of real love. They evaporate when the light of real life hits and are worth little in the real world. Heightened emotions and verbal promises left in limbo serve only to deepen animosity between people. Love must be proved in substantive action, as Scripture shows us in 2 Corinthians 8—9. Jesus' love—by which the world is to know we are believers—was costly and sacrificial. It meant a relinquishing of power; it meant humility; it meant a coming and dwelling among people. It *was* relational. But warm feelings alone are the sentiment of love without the courage or thoughtfulness to give it substance—a cowardly lion or thoughtless scarecrow in the light of the kingdom.

If the civil rights movement, Reconstruction and the Civil War should teach us anything, they should teach us that you cannot make someone love you by waging a war or passing legislation. Such efforts may help to restrain evil, but they do not engender love between people. Truth be told, they either expose and exacerbate open animosity or force it underground. They may be right and necessary; they may be needed to improve the life of some. However, they are but hollow shells of real love. They are the form of love without its lifeblood—a tin man with no substance, no heart.

In pursuit of justice, we must have both a relational and a power-based approach. We need to have actual love for both oppressor and oppressed, and we need to not be satisfied with hugs and handshakes.

Since we live in a fallen, sinful world, we will need law and such, but they cannot substitute for kingdom love. In truth, if we all loved with God's love, there would be no need for the huge legal system we have today.

BEING A BRIDGE PERSON

All God's people are called to be bridge people, people who cross over ethnic, cultural and class lines to bring the good news of the gospel in word and deed. Jesus demonstrates his great freedom to cross ethnic lines as he visits with Samaritans and ministers to Gentiles. Peter finally gets the message in Acts 10—11. And then Paul, the great early church missionary, makes it plain in his journeys and teachings: Galatians 2 and 1 Corinthians 9:19-23 are good representative examples.

We are all, by definition, given the role and responsibility of crossing such lines, both evangelistically and among believers. Jesus' teaching in John 17 is the clearest portrayal of this. He says that all believers are to be as one, intimately connected, like a loving family, so that the world will know that he came from the Father. The unity of believers is not only commanded in 1 Corinthians 12 as expressing the identity of the church. Nor is it only used by Jesus to characterize the family of God. Our unity is said to be the means, the determining, authenticating sign, that Jesus was sent by God. Not only so, but it is called the identifying mark of any believer. They will indeed know if we are Christians by our love.

As Paul the evangelist exemplifies through his labor to simultaneously get the gospel out and call the believing community to unity, there can be no separation of concern for evangelism and unity in the church. In fact, Jesus' prayer in John 17 implies that demonstrations of unity are in some sense evangelistic. They tell people of the world who Jesus is. Why? Because there is no other reason that people who hated each other in the world would now be together and be loving one another sacrificially. Is it any wonder then that many revivals have come about as believers, in humility, chose unity and prayed, labored, lived, worshiped and shared economic resources? The Holy Spirit has come in power and many have come to know God. The Azusa Street Revival and others around the world, particularly in the last decades, bear witness to this.

A friend of mine, Maria, is an immigrant from Latin America. Like virtually every willing immigrant in the history of the United States, she came with the hope of working and making a better life for her and her family. She worked for years cleaning other people's floors, washing their windows, keeping their homes nice, in order to raise her kids and purchase her own home. After her boys were grown, she came into contact with a group of people who were different from any others she had known. They were like family, yet they were unrelated. They ate together, were very concerned for each other's well-being and were committed to helping each other out financially. They enjoyed being with each other, and they were very open and welcoming to her and others. It was not an episode of *Friends* or *Seinfeld*. It was not a friendship clique. It was real people with real lives, with real problems and apparently real love for each other.

Yet these folks were very different from her and from each other. There were ethnic differences: one black, one Indian, five Anglos, two Japanese, one Chinese, one Latina. Others joined them later: a Samoan, a Sri Lankan, a Mexican, a Korean, another Chinese woman, three more Anglos and two blacks. There were some economic differences as well.

What is happening here? Maria said to this group, "You all seem like family to me." And so it was. They labored to be family together, to live out the truth of Jesus' words as a witness. It was compelling for her. Having grown up in church, she now experienced a new faith life, her own personal revival. And she too was woven into the relational fabric of the group. What drew Maria to this group, and kept her there, was the love of God expressed in the unity of believers.

Christians' unity witnesses to who Jesus is. Why then have we chosen to be so divisive? Divisive denominational lives would be enough of a concern. But the church is also divided by class and race. We are a sad example of unity—the mirror is so cracked that the world can't see who Jesus is at times. We have been a poor witness.

John Perkins has had a prophetic vision for the church's reconciliation and unity. Too often that vision has been ignored, but today some fellowships have committed themselves to reconciliation out of obedience to Jesus. For example:

- Rock Church in Chicago is laboring to hold out this witness. This fellowship has historically been a place for black and white believers to build unity and has engaged in substantial work for those in need. People who have struggled economically and others who have substantial means are part of the fellowship together.

- Evergreen Church in Los Angeles is making a deliberate effort to pray and work to head more in this direction. This historically Japanese church is now more broadly Asian, with other ethnic groups present. Its members are taking a hard look at following God's call to become more diverse across economic and racial lines as well as other social barriers. While historically committed to overseas missions, in recent years they have begun ministering to those in need in their immediate neighborhood.

- Faith Christian Fellowship in Baltimore has committed itself to justice and reconciliation. Sunday mornings reveal a pretty diverse congregation gathered for worship. But the church's labor during the week gives even more evidence of God's grace. They have started a small school and have dealt with economic and ethnic barriers for some time now.

Whether our local body of believers has taken large steps toward reconciliation or only baby steps thus far, the issue is where we are going. In what direction are we headed? How are we praying and relating to fellow believers and to those outside the faith?

The gospel is fundamentally relational in nature, and therefore in a sense we are all called to be bridge people. As we pursue justice, authentic relationships must develop across racial and class divisions. We must step out across these barriers and not simply accept them. We must be the church in all its fullness. Our birthright as believers is nothing less.

DEALING WITH POWER

All God's people are called to deal with power. Now there are several ways to understand this. By the witness of the ministry of the Holy Spirit in the New Testament, apparently all believers are to minister in power, resist the power of the world and walk in victory, defeating the power of the devil. For us to resist the power of the world, to actually defeat the power of the devil, a power has to be at work within us and through us that is greater than these, that brings us into conflict with the world and the devil and compels us in a different direction. The power of God in the presence of the Holy Spirit can keep us from the love of money and enable all forms of healing and deliverance ministry. Throughout church history, Christians have found different ways to relate to the power of the world and of the devil. Scripture itself contains a couple of models for how to deal with power.

Reformers use worldly power to effect change, sometimes for great good. Scriptural examples include the Old Testament kings who sought to exercise governing authority with wisdom. Joseph is another model. From slavery followed by imprisonment under false charges (only one strike was allowed in those days), he rose to take a prominent position in an ungodly, secular government. Reformers occupy a key position within a power structure and wield power in ways that bless many people and move forward God's purposes in the world. They have opportunities to shape structures and laws or mold the application of these laws. They can appoint others to faithfully serve in certain positions. They are faithful witnesses in their respective contexts.

Separatists, on the other hand, renounce the use of worldly power themselves and call those who are using it to account. They speak to those in power and call them to act justly, to repent, to do what is right in the eyes of the Lord. Though they also call the broader people of God to reform, they don't exercise governing authority or hold office. Some of them come from pretty odd backgrounds (like shepherding—Amos) or are young (Jeremiah) to have such clear perspective and speak with such authority to those who wield power. Often in their time there is no lasting response or revival. These are the prophets. They too are faithful witnesses.

These distinctions blur in some biblical characters like Moses and Samuel. Sometimes people's roles change over the course of their ministry. Moses first is a prophetic type with Pharaoh and then has the role of a reformer as he leads the Israelites as their first judge. Samuel has the role of judge at times and prophet at others.

What is significant is that both are represented in the Bible. The reformers took opportunities that were available to them to wield authority. The prophets, who most often were called by God in times of faithlessness, generally had no role available within the governing structure, and so they called for reform from the outside. At their best times, reformers and separatists worked in concert. The prophets brought correction, offered encouragement and gave direction to those who held positions of power. Those in power sought the advice of the prophets.

One thing is clear: God's people are called to deal with power. The opportunities and tactics may change depending on our situation, gifting and calling, but we must deal with it. Sometimes the Davids kill the Uriahs and must be exposed and called to repentance. Sometimes the Jezebels and Ahabs steal from the Naboths. Sometimes those in power take advantage of those who are governed. Sometimes they lord it over those they lead. It should not be so among the people of God. It is not so in God's kingdom.

We must see that justice is secured for those who have been wronged, looking after and protecting the interests of those who do not have a voice within the system. And we must deal with power, because sometimes the leaders of an organization need guidance and will give us the opportunity to bring God's wisdom and blessing into a crisis. Sometimes Pharaoh needs Joseph and will call on him to help the nation out.

At one point Maria was looking for a way for her two sons to be employed. After thinking about this for a while, she thought of taking out a loan on her little house and purchasing a small lot next door. It was a good place for a small tire shop, and her sons could work there and make a living. She secured the loan and was asked to put up her home as collateral. Since she had paid off her initial mortgage, she figured that between her income and her sons' she would have no trouble paying off the loan. She signed the papers, and the seller instructed her to make her payments to a representative. For several years she made regular payments to this man. Then suddenly one day she received a notice that her property was being foreclosed on by the seller, who had financed the deal and held the mortgage, because she was delinquent in her payments.

As it turned out, for many months the representative had not given Maria's payments to the seller. She had paid cash. There were no receipts.

The wealthy landowner sued for return of the lot and ownership of her house. Maria's lawyer, who initially had been very keen to take on her case, suddenly got interested in running for political office. As the trial approached, he did relatively little to prepare and would not listen to the prophetic witness of believers who sought to stir him to action. So he was also, in part, responsible for the outcome.

The judge ruled in the seller's favor, finding Maria to be a shrewd opportunist instead of a trusting woman who believed what she was told, held to her commitments and was taken advantage of. Even in our day, there are Ahabs who steal from the Naboths.

Though some believers came to Maria's aid, testified on her behalf and worked to speak truth in the situation, she lost her home. Sometimes the prophetic witness goes unheard; there is no repentance, no revival.

We may not always be able to bring about justice, but we must deal with power. And then we stand by those who suffer because of an unfair ruling. There was a believing community that prayed with Maria and her family and walked with them through this process and afterward. A Christian businessman who owned a nearby property leased an apartment to her at a below-market rate. And Maria walked on, bruised but cared for, in faith. She thanked God that she had the house and business long enough to raise her two sons. Like Job she would say, "The Lord giveth, and the Lord taketh away. Blessed be the name of the Lord" (see Job 1:21).

ONE LAST PIECE

Truth be told, if a ministry exclusively addressed cases of injustice, even in a scriptural way, it would be incomplete. Practical social service work is needed, but a significant number of organizations are doing such work, while only very few are concerned with developing *worshiping communities* among the poor, which then address instances of injustice in ways appropriate to the context. Immense poverty belts surround the world's major urban centers, and frequently within them there is little (if any) witness of the gospel, no church. Many residents of these areas have never even heard Jesus' name.

As I read the New Testament, as I consider Jesus' life and ministry, and as I look at Paul, I conclude that it is not enough to reach out and minister to the needs of the poor. We must hope and labor for the planting of fellowships of believers who will live in these areas and be the body of Christ with and for the people there. These fellowships will address the needs around them, but they will most centrally minister to people's need to know God.

Like Jesus, we must be concerned for the whole person. Even if our work is successful in transforming society, in the overall scheme of things that success will be short lived. History has proved it so. So even as we labor toward more just relationships and a more just society, we recognize that these changes will be complete and permanent only in the full coming of the kingdom.

8

A LIFE OF JUSTICE

SOCRATES ONCE STATED that the unexamined life is not worth living. Though that is a hyperbolic statement, it remains true that a person of faith is constantly called into reflection on the practices of her life in following Jesus. For the Lord is always offering us his testimony, his Word, his model as a challenge to the way we are doing things, to the way we think, feel and behave. Over time, those of us who follow him must allow our assumptions, values and practices to be challenged and, if need be, changed by the Lord.

As we reflect on our practice of justice and love for those in need, we do well to focus our critique first on our own life and not on others or on society. Though having a broad view of our times is good and it is entirely appropriate to consider the faithfulness of various trends and decisions in our workplace and neighborhood, the first order of business is always to deal with ourselves.

We are not able to remove the splinter from another's eye, says Jesus, while having a log in our own. So he offers this advice: "First take the log out of your own eye, and then you will see clearly to take out the speck that is in your brother's eye" (Luke 6:42). It isn't that the blindness of my neighbor is unimportant. It should be dealt with, and in love, in time, I will offer my assistance—seeing what they cannot see and removing that which hurts them. This concern for my neighbor is important; but in order to be of any assistance, I need to get right first.

Now we may take offense at the suggestion that we have a log in our eye while our neighbor has only a splinter. But only a thorough examination will show us our log, and it is in our best interest to look closely and seek out the change and healing that we need. An old adage offers the same wisdom: "You can't lead anyone where you haven't been." Until God has done substantial work in us, until we have taken some steps, we should be reticent to comment negatively on the actions of others. Our growth in zeal should be matched with a growth in wisdom. And this is never a fully done process. We need to always be open to learn from Jesus and follow his leading.

To that end, here are a few arenas to explore.

SPENDING

How much money do you spend on things that you don't actually need? For example, if you are a college student and have a meal plan that's paid for, how much do you spend to eat out—in effect paying for the same meal twice? How much do you spend on entertainment—whether CDs, movies or the newest electronic gadgets? Do you buy extra clothes and shoes just because they're fashionable, not because you need them?

Many pastors preach about the financial riches promised to those who believe. Scripture, of course, is fundamentally at odds with such messages. It's more faithful to ask, "If I have money, how does God want me to use it?" See if that's addressed next time you hear a sermon on the riches God promises us in this life. According to Scripture, we are no more free to do whatever we want with our money than we are to use our body to sleep around. The Bible offers pretty clear guidelines for both.

John Wesley, whose ministry was used by God to generate the Methodist revival, came home to his residence at Oxford University one day, having just bought some pictures for his room. At his door he found one of the women who cleaned the residence. It was a cold winter day, and he noticed that she only had thin clothing to wear. He resolved to give her some money for a coat, but when he reached for his cash he found he had little to offer. She went on her way with nothing.

While some people might not have even thought twice about the situation, Wesley was saddened by his inability to give and recokoned it a mark of poor stewardship on his part that he was unprepared. He was convicted that the Lord was not pleased with how he had used his money. He had spent his money needlessly on the pictures that he had desired, and so could not help one whom God loved and put in his path that day.

Wesley did not just go away sorrowful; he resolved to rethink and rework his finances. After this, for the better part of his life he lived on the same amount of income that he began with. In other words, though his income increased, he chose to keep his standard of living and his lifestyle at the original level. Biographer Charles White tells us that Wesley believed that "with increasing income, the Christian's standard of giving should increase, not his standard of living." The fact that he could afford something was no indication that he should purchase it. Rather, he lived simply, saved what he could have spent on luxuries and comforts for himself, and gave all that he had left over to meet the needs of others (story originally told in *Faith on the Edge,* pp. 137-38).

Jesus tells a story in Luke 16 that brings Wesley's thinking into sharp relief:

> There was a rich man, who was clothed in purple and fine linen and who feasted sumptuously every day. And at his gate lay a poor man named Laz'arus, full of sores, who desired to be fed with what fell from the rich man's table; moreover the dogs came and licked his sores. The poor man died and was carried by the angels to Abraham's bosom. The rich man also died and was buried; and in Hades, being in torment, he lifted up his eyes, and saw Abraham far off and Laz'arus in his bosom. And he called out, "Father Abraham, have mercy upon me, and send Laz'arus to dip the end of his finger in water and cool my tongue; for I am in anguish in this flame." But

Abraham said, "Son, remember that you in your lifetime received your good things, and Laz'arus in like manner evil things; but now he is comforted here, and you are in anguish. And besides all this, between us and you a great chasm has been fixed, in order that those who would pass from here to you may not be able, and none may cross from there to us." And he said, "Then I beg you, father, to send him to my father's house, for I have five brothers, so that he may warn them, lest they also come into this place of torment." But Abraham said, "They have Moses and the prophets; let them hear them." And he said, "No, father Abraham; but if some one goes to them from the dead, they will repent." He said to him, "If they do not hear Moses and the prophets, neither will they be convinced if someone should rise from the dead." (verses 19-31)

Though the circumstances of their lives and the decisions that they faced were the same, the response of the rich man to the needs of those around him and the direction of his life are the opposite of Wesley's.

STANDARD OF LIVING

Have you decided on a certain standard of living? For example: Do you envision yourself in a certain type of home, with certain belongings, in a certain type of job or neighborhood? Is that a biblical vision of your future or a culturally and family generated version? What does the Word teach us about how we should live, what we should have and what goals we should set? This is important, since whether we acknowledge it or not, the hopes and dreams that we cherish will shape us and the decisions we make.

Like Wesley, consider undertaking a vow to live simply. No rigid standard can be used to determine a simple lifestyle, given the different costs of living in different parts of the world. And as always, there is a range of ways to apply this value in the gospel. The idea is not to cultivate austerity for its own sake but to live simply in order to save money for other things—acts of generosity.

It can help to track your spending for a short time and then use that information as the basis for establishing a budget to live within. You may decide to fast from some luxury item that is unneeded. Before undertaking any substantial purchase, practice a discipline of prayer and self-examination. The appendix lists some resources to help you explore the possibilities.

GETTING CLOSE TO THE POOR

Are you committed to giving to the poor and building relationships with those in need? Budgeting your money or giving to a hunger relief program is a fine step. But actually knowing someone who is poor and seeing what they have to deal with is a different matter. Choosing to help someone by offering them some of your food or clothing, as John the Baptist encourages (see Luke 3:11), forces a greater recognition of the person's humanity. And it is far more personal to give a piece of clothing that is yours than to write a check to an organization whose staff you have never met to serve a person you will never meet.

A number of organizations are doing good work in ministering to the poor, and we should support those efforts. But we should also seek to respond more personally. In the process we will find that many popular stereotypes of the poor or of certain ethnic groups will be challenged, as will our understanding of why people are in these situations.

RELEARNING HISTORY

Do you have a balanced view of your nation's history, the history of your city, the history of the institutions to which you belong? For example: Have you been taught to love your country uncritically or to see it clearly in light of Scripture's standards of goodness, righteousness and justice? If you are an American, are you aware of some of the uglier parts of our history—sometimes unethical policies of the U.S. government, both at home and abroad?

I was taught to love our country, and I do. But I was not taught to evaluate it and see it clearly. I was not taught the uglier parts of our history, with the exception of slavery and certain parts of the mid-twentieth century—and even these accounts were fairly sanitized. Love does not require a lack of critique. In fact, real love will offer constructive critique where it is needed. We must see our times clearly to know what the gospel has to say about the world we live in. Asking God to give us a balanced view and some concrete examples and experiences to work with is important. The appendix lists some resources to help you here.

READING SCRIPTURE

Are you able to study Scripture and understand it without an economic class bias? Are you familiar with the many passages that teach about or demonstrate God's concern for the poor? If your answer to the first question is yes, be careful. For we all read the Bible (and anything else) through our own cultural and class experience in some measure. We need the Spirit of God and people of other backgrounds to help us see clearly.

There are many possible places to start considering the Bible's teaching about the poor. The books of the Law include substantive passages on the topic, and the exodus of the Hebrews from slavery in Egypt can provide us with insight into God's heart. The Old Testament histories give compelling testimony to the elite's lack of concern for the poor. Ahab's stealing of Naboth's vineyard is a stirring picture of a corrupt leader exploiting people for personal gain. The Wisdom literature includes much commentary on those in need. The prophets regularly denounce the abuse of the poor.

The Gospels tell us of a Messiah who came from a poor family, was born in a barn, fled as an international refugee and later ministered as a homeless man supported by the gifts of his followers. It is the most compelling picture of God's commitment to and identification with the poor. He came as one of them, relinquishing the grandeur and glory that had been his. He even left the security of his family and trade. He was a nobody ministering to nobodies, just like any other Juan or Maria born in a small town and growing up in a cultural backwater. And this is part of the glory of God, that he would choose to come in such a way, to see us and to live in difficult circumstances. Such is the path, the call and the witness to humanity. Such is the path of humility, of simplicity and of refusal to demand what might even rightfully be ours. Such is the path of Christ. The gate is indeed narrow and the way is hard that leads to eternal life, and those who find it are few. Jesus urges us, "Strive to enter by the narrow door" (Luke 13:24).

Suggestions

1. Try keeping track of how you spend your money for a month or two. Then actually try making a budget. It makes sense to understand where your money goes and how it gets there before you seek to direct its use.

2. Try doing a word study on the topic of the poor in Scripture. If you can find it in print, Ron Sider has a helpful listing of these Scriptures along with succinct interpretive work in his book *Cry Justice*.

3. Try fasting from entertainment with a friend for a month and give what you would have spent toward caring for someone—an individual or a family—in need.

John Wesley had a pithy teaching on believers' use of money: they should earn all they can, save all they can and give all they can. In the Methodist revival, many who had been poor heeded the first two points and improved their lot. But instead of giving generously, they became wealthy. Wesley believed that it was the Lord's displeasure with this that quenched the revival. We would do well to follow all three steps.

The first part of the chapter points us toward personal evaluation and change. But there is more, Finding some brothers and sisters to work through these things with and walking together with them is essential.

FINDING PARTNERS

Jesus tells us that we will always have the poor with us (Mark 14:7). There will always be new opportunities to love and serve. Given the way the world works, until God makes all things new there will always be plenty of work to address poverty and injustice. This realization may kill the romanticism of our "change the world" drive. However, if we are involved in justice work for long, we recognize that indeed the world will be changed, and the Lord will do it in part through each of us; but the world will not become a fully just place, and there will be cruel and unjust people and systems within it until the Lord comes. This should not discourage us. Rather, it should focus us on the task at hand in the proclamation of the kingdom.

By following Jesus, walking in his steps, we move into this work, which is part of the labor of the church over the generations. We are part of a long line of prophets, of witnesses, who have come announcing the good news that Jesus proclaimed and demonstrating that good news to the world, and particularly to those in need.

And we should enter this work together. Finding partners for the journey is one of the most significant steps you can take as you begin to craft a life of justice and concern for the poor. Scripture pictures the life of faith as a journey, and along the way we will continually be learning. In this sense we will never really be done, or finished, in terms of learning and growing in becoming people who follow God's call to live justly and righteously.

It is worth remembering that the texts of the Old and New Testaments were written primarily to groups of people and not to individuals. Part of the lost wisdom of our time in the United States is how to actually be a spiritual community—to respond to the issues of our times *together.* Individual response is important, but so is communal response. We can seek the counsel of others as we examine our personal use of money and lifestyle choices. We should look to learn together with others about the world and gain a sense of Jesus' leading.

We are made to have partners in life: people with whom we walk through life, people who encourage, support and challenge us, people whom we encourage, support and challenge. Scripture rarely pictures a Lone Ranger kind of Christian. Rather, it testifies to the need and compelling beauty of a community of faith that loves as Jesus did.

What contemporary social trends prevent people from building deep relationships and rooting themselves in a shared life as God's people? Cultural individualism, relativism and the relative transience of our society certainly don't help us. Still, by God's grace we can find partners to help us and whom we will help along the way. We simply must stay committed to the adventure, stay put long enough and accept the discipline we need from the Lord to become who we were made to be.

WITNESSES

Several years ago, a few friends decided they were not happy with their personal use of money and how they handled certain financial decisions. Rather than visiting a financial planner, they decided to look at the Bible and see how the Lord would counsel them first. From Scripture they gained an excellent view of giving, saving, insurance, spending, investments and other issues, and this provided a framework within which to discuss decisions with each other. They opened up their spending records and shared the details with one another. Critique was welcomed.

How many people do you know who offer an open audit of their finances? Not exactly a common practice in the United States.

Today these friends continue to have much to say about all the ways God is teaching them and growing them. God has led them to jointly become involved in refugee ministry and to "adopt" a particular family, meeting their needs during their transition into a new culture and new challenges. They have also made interesting personal decisions. One has formed a family foundation for charitable giving to the poor, with a focus on the AIDS crisis overseas. Another couple helps to lead a summer internship that brings college students to the poorer areas of their city, where they learn from people who are ministering there year round.

This is a form of biblical community. Find some partners who really want to learn and grow and begin to explore what God has to teach you together. Learn together, respond together and respond personally.

BECOMING INFORMED

In addition to gaining some partners in the process, gaining a clearer picture of how the world works and what is really going on is an important step. In the end, we will be praised or chastised not for how well we know history but for how we have responded to and lived in our own times. One could spend infinite days in research of history and actually do nothing with the knowledge. Some historical investigation is necessary to understand why some things are the way they are—only then can we discern appropriate solutions. But the need for current information about both local and global issues is most essential.

Be discerning; cultivate an inquiring mind. Statistics can be collected to support almost any outcome. When you're reading reports that cite statistics from social research, consider carefully the kinds of surveys that were taken, the kinds of questions that were asked and the kinds of people who were polled.

Cultivate a broad network of friendships with people of various ethnic and economic backgrounds. Learn about their culture and experiences. Part of becoming informed will mean getting to know people who are very different and learning to build informed friendship.

Consider taking some focused time to learn and be mentored by people who are engaged in some kind of justice ministry year round. For college students, one such option is one of InterVarsity Christian Fellowship's urban projects or its Global Urban Trek. These range from a weekend to eight weeks in length. They are intensive "urban seminaries" packed with study, ministry and community building. Servant Partners has a short-term international practicum and a longer domestic version. Participants may be adults of any age. World Impact, Mission Year and InnerCHANGE also offer some appropriate programs, or you may wish to do an internship or an extended volunteer stint with a Christian relief agency or a ministry close to home.

HAVE NO POLITICAL LEANING

This is difficult for many of us, for we want to see the world the way we already see it. We don't like certain facts, since they might cause us to change our view of the world, of a legislative agenda or of a certain leader. But if we cling to our preferences, we'll miss the truth.

If a once-favored policy or person is not getting the job done, objectivity and detachment will permit us to recognize the problem, voice our concern and seek a better solution. The gospel is neither Democratic nor Republican, nor does it have any particular political affiliation. It is good news in *any* society with *any* style of government or economic system. Inherent in the gospel is also a sharp critique of any political system, since by nature it will be fallen just as the people who serve in it are fallen.

DON'T GET OBSESSED

Seeking justice can become an all-consuming task. Be patient and just keep working at it along with your group of explorers. After a while, you will find some resources more reliable than others. These must also still be questioned periodically, but when a source proves to be trustworthy over time, make full use of it.

Evangelicals for Social Action has proved a valuable resource for many. I encourage you to investigate the organization and its publications. I believe it may be useful to you. I have also frequently enjoyed the company and writings of the Jesuits and the Franciscans. Other branches of the church also have gifts to offer.

A LAST NOTE

As Jesus leads us into a life of seeking justice, we will discover a means of meaningful civic participation, having a voice in our society and growing in personal integrity. We are called away from apathy and into hope. For we know both who reigns and who will reign—and it is our birthright to participate in the glorious coming of his kingdom. We should not settle for less.

As Jesus' body, the church, his physical presence on earth, we stand and announce, even as he did, "The Spirit of the Lord is upon us, because he has anointed us to preach good news to the poor. He has sent us to proclaim release to the captives and recovering of sight to the blind, to set at liberty those who are oppressed, to proclaim the acceptable year of the Lord" (see Luke 4:18-19). Indeed, in every place that believers are, this message should resound—for still today, this Scripture is fulfilled in those who truly hear.

9

THE COMING OF TROUBLE

SCRIPTURE IS VERY CLEAR about this in both direct teaching and the example of what happens to godly people in the Bible. There will be trouble—persecution, trials, ridicule, threats. When it comes, it should not surprise us or dissuade us from our ministry. People, structures and spiritual forces will oppose the work of God, and therefore they will oppose the people involved in the work.

Of course we may face opposition for any of a variety of reasons. We may, in the pursuit of justice, do something wrong. We may sin against someone or some group. We may have lacked discernment, and so we failed to love when we had opportunity. The trick is this: we must not allow persecution for the sake of the gospel to dissuade us from following Jesus, and yet we have to heed the truly wise rebuke and prophetic critique. We must not shrink back in response to unjust opposition, yet we must not blindly reject all criticism.

We also will face personal trials along the way. These involve persecution when various spiritual forces seek to attack God's work by attacking us personally. Or our trials may simply be ways in which our character flaws and sin issues get tested.

One friend runs a nonprofit ministry that partners with a local church to bring educational assistance into a poor neighborhood. Over the years he has faced frequent funding challenges. These have affected him personally, since the ministry provides salaries for him and a few part-time staff. If the funds run out, he will not have money to pay the bills and put food on the table in his home. It is difficult to walk through such trials in faith. Today he is still there, the ministry is flourishing, and the funding has stabilized for the time being. But the real testimony is found not in present funding successes but in the faith and character that grew in him as he walked through those trials with God.

I am now thirty-eight years old, and up until two months ago I was single. In the midst of trying to follow God into ministry, one personal challenge was very straightforward for me: *will I ever find a partner and marry?* A history of struggles with sexual lust, a busy schedule and a challenging ministry environment did not bode well for my chances of building a healthy romantic relationship. To be frank, the fishing pond had gotten rather small, and as I got older it seemed it would shrink more. I had to decide multiple times whether I was willing to follow God even if it meant that I might be single for life. Should I change ministries or do something else for a living? I had regular seasons of these challenges. The question was clear: Was there a price at which I could be bought? Was there something that could induce me to abandon the call and ministry God had given me?

CAN I BE BOUGHT?

Let's say a big-time corporate businessman walked up to you and said, "I've got a great job for you. It's high-end investment banking, and you will start out on top with a million-dollar salary."

That might feel good. But you'd probably want a few specifics, and so you inquire. He says, "Well you would work normal industry hours, maybe seventy per week on average, and have little time for your family, but remember, I could offer you a million."

You agree, figuring, *What the heck, I'll take it for only a short time and then I'll retire.* So you tell him OK.

Then he comes back at you and clarifies further: "Well, the salary might not be that good. Would you be willing to do it for a dollar?"

You would of course be indignant and probably say something like "That's ridiculous—what kind of person do you think I am?" Great question. Many corporate lawyers call the first few years they work for a firm the "whore years"—and for good reason.

A friend of mine put it in a different parable form. A guy walks into a bar and sees a woman he finds very attractive. He walks up to her, talks with her some, and they have a couple of drinks together. Then he turns to her and asks, "Would you sleep with me for a million dollars?"

Surprised, she thinks for a minute and responds, "Sure."

He waits for a minute and then asks, "So . . . would you sleep with me for a dollar?"

She reacts with indignation: "Of course not! What kind of a woman do you think I am?"

He replies coolly, "We've already determined that; now we're just discussing the price."

Not a pretty picture. But the challenge we face is just that real. If there is a price at which we can be bought, the world and the enemy will find it. And the fee paid will be as low as we're willing to go—the enemy will not offer any more incentives than are necessary.

If we were to contextualize the temptations of Jesus into justice ministry in our day, the story might read something like this:

After being anointed for ministry among the poor, she was led into the wilderness of the urban jungle, a life of simplicity and humility for ten years; and when they had ended, she was lonely. And the devil came to her and said, "If you are a daughter of God, leave and find a husband; there are many men in the suburbs."

She answered him, "It is written, 'Your Maker is your husband, the Lord of hosts is his name.'"

Then the devil showed her in a moment all the grandeur of the life and times of the rich and famous. And he said, "All this is mine, and I give it to whomever I choose. If you then will worship me, it shall be yours."

She replied, "It is written, 'A person's life does not consist in the abundance of her possessions.'"

Then the devil took her to the dangerous house on her block where drug deals and shootings were common. And he said, "If you are a daughter of God, enter here and claim this place for the kingdom. Clear out the inhabitants and take possession of it, for it is written, 'Be strong and courageous. . . . Every place that the sole of your foot will tread upon I have given to you'; and 'No weapon that is fashioned against you shall prosper.'"

She answered him, "It is said, 'Not by might, nor by power, but by my Spirit, says the Lord'; and again, 'The zeal of the Lord of hosts will do this.'"

And when the devil had ended these temptations, he departed from her, until an opportune time.

Such are the challenges of a person who would follow Jesus into a ministry that deals in a direct, incarnational way with the poor. The devil is not done with her, just done for now.

But the story of course does not end there; it would continue with something like *And she returned in the power of the Holy Spirit . . .* The Lord will work, and we will see his blessing and provision, if we can but stand fast in the midst of the battle against the wiles of the enemy.

As we face personal trials, we do well to embrace the struggle rather than evade it. In the words of James, we should consider it all joy when we encounter various trials, because the testing of our faith will produce steadfastness. And let steadfastness have its full effect, so that we may be perfect and complete, lacking nothing (James 1:2-4). Jesus says that we are blessed—to be envied!—when people revile us and persecute us falsely on his account. We should rejoice and be glad, for our reward is great in heaven, for so people persecuted the prophets who were before us (Matthew 5:11-12). Let us press on to know the Lord in his sufferings, and let us equip ourselves with the Word, prayer and community to stand fast in the battles we will face. And let us allow the work of the Holy Spirit in us to purify us through these experiences, so that we may indeed be lacking nothing.

THE NEED FOR PRAYER AND DISCERNMENT

In chapter seven I noted that there are predatory forces that seek the lives of the poor. Recounting his early experiences of working among the poor, William Stringfellow says,

> Slowly I learned something which folk indigenous to the ghetto know: namely, that the power and purpose of death are incarnated in the institutions and structures, procedures and regimes— Consolidated Edison or the Department of Welfare, the Mafia or the police, the Housing Authority or the social work bureaucracy, the hospital system or the banks, liberal philanthropy or corporate real estate speculation. In the wisdom of the people of the East Harlem neighborhood, such principalities are identified as demonic powers. (*Instead of Death*, 1967 ed., quoted in Bill Wylie-Kellermann, "Resisting Death Incarnate," *Sojourners*, March/April 1996, p. 1)

Bill Wylie-Kellermann reflects thus on Stringfellow's discovery of the spiritual forces behind poverty:

> Where churches begin to engage the violence now invading and occupying our own urban neighborhoods, a theological analysis of the principalities and powers may prove crucial. On the one hand, it enables a biblical way of naming and thereby seeing what is sometimes called the "structural violence" targeted with uncanny vitality against the urban poor. And on the other, it explains like nothing else, the street-level violence (now mushrooming out of control) that people turn upon one another. And beyond both, it may suggest certain spiritual resources the church must claim in this struggle which truly "is not against flesh and blood, but against powers and principalities, against powers, against rulers of the darkness of the world, against spiritual wickedness in the heavenly places." ("Resisting Death Incarnate," *Sojourners*, March/April 1996, p. 1)

This topic merits discussion at some length, more than I can provide in this book. The spiritual roots of poverty and oppression must be dealt with as we move out to act. Let us pray and discern together the nature of these roots in our community and in our country. Some people have been at work at this already for many years, and we can benefit from their wisdom and pray on. But note well, any effort to deal with spiritual forces by human means alone will not suffice. The forces that are allied against us are too great. We must press into God before and during our labors. If he moves, there are none that can withstand him.

Further resources for exploring this struggle are listed in the appendix.

PATIENCE AND PERSISTENCE

Speed is valued in our society. Time is of the essence. People make millions from just being able to do something faster. Within any organization, efficiency and productivity are central. This is business thinking, but it can seep into the church. Numbers, stats and development can become unhealthy concerns for us. When we begin to define our success in the world's terms, we become overly concerned with achieving quick and quantifiable results.

Our true success consists in remaining faithful to the work God has called us to do, being who he has called us to be in the world. Of course we hope that people will respond to our efforts and that structures will indeed be reformed. It may happen quickly or take years before any substantial change can be seen. In some cases it may never happen.

Through the centuries chronicled in the Old Testament, a series of prophets issued calls for reform. They all failed. There was little to no response. There was opposition and persecution. People were killed. And over the long term, people and institutions did not change. So over generations, God waited patiently, giving plenty of opportunity for his people to respond. After this season, he gradually brought a judgment for their lack of obedience, repentance, justice and righteousness.

Were the prophets failures? In worldly terms, yes. It was a noble failure, something to be admired—from a distance.

But a broader, more godly perspective would hold that though the prophets did fail to inspire the reforms they hoped for, they did not fail to minister the word of God in the situations of their day. They did not fail to live differently from those around them. They did not fail to speak the truth to power. They called the establishment to account.

Jesus inspired no great reform in his day. At the end of his life, it seemed that his movement was suffering the fate of many other prophetic movements and revivals: the leader gets killed, the followers are repressed, and the whole thing fades away on a sad and sour note. But Jesus' death was far from a failure, for in the economy of God, nothing goes to waste. Though they struck Jesus down, he became more powerful than his enemies could possibly imagine. And after fifty days or so, the revolution from down under simply grew in numbers and power. In the long run, it was more than Rome could handle.

Are we willing to be one in a line of people who minister to the poor and suffering of the world, content to labor and let God bring the harvest, whether in our time or later? Or are we just in this because it's an adventure, or a job, or something our friends are doing? Is it because we regularly get to see victories? Or because it's the call of God and we are willing to accept the suffering and costs that come with the great blessings of life with God? Or are we fair-weather shepherds who run at the sign of trouble, inconvenience and lack of results? Someone has said that there are two gifts that no one asks for in believing communities these days: singleness and martyrdom. We may not ask for them, but will we accept them if they are brought to us by the Lord's hand?

Patience and persistence are necessary in this work if we are to last in it or see the fruit that is hoped for. Patience is needed because it takes time for us and any other people to change. Sometimes there are amazing growth spurts in spiritual life, but much lasting development comes more slowly. Character takes time to form.

Patience is needed because love requires that we allow others to grow and respond as the Holy Spirit inspires and not at the rate we might prefer. Such is spiritual life. Jesus, living in an agricultural society, used this image: "If a man should scatter seed upon the ground, and should sleep and rise night and day, and the seed should sprout and grow, he knows not how" (Mark 4:26-27). We must be content to labor and let God bring growth as he chooses in us, in others and in the society around us.

Persistence is needed because if we are not constant and thorough in our work, it will be subverted by the current of the world. Jesus was, if anything, persistent with his proclamation of the kingdom, constant in his training of the Twelve, regular in his denunciation of corrupt spirituality and thorough in his modeling of love for those in need. Personal and structural reform take time, and we must be patient and persistent, not spotty in our efforts to bring about change. Our work must be steady.

Here is a history lesson of one American man who had both patience and persistence and saw gradual change over time. John Woolman was a Quaker by faith. He came under the conviction that slavery was a moral sin and that no person should own slaves. Though many of his friends and associates disagreed, he was not to be dissuaded. He spent years of his life riding from town to town, talking to every Quaker he could. Gradually he persuaded each of them that slavery was a moral sin and to own slaves was to sin against God. By the end of his labors, no Quaker owned slaves. Some actually gave their slaves economic resources as they released them. Nearly a century before the Civil War, this man had accomplished by words and prayer what we could not settle as a nation with votes and guns. Sometimes patience, persistence and persuasion are able to accomplish a great deal in the Lord's hands.

We may see revival and reform in our day. We may see gradual progress. We may see no significant reform. But let us be clear about this. The question at the end of the day will be about how we have lived and whom we have followed. It will be about whom we have believed and how we have given evidence of that in our lives. You won't be asked about the numbers, the projects or the stats. You will be asked whom you know. So let us give ourselves with both patience and persistence to the labor we are given by the Lord, that we may know him and be known by him when we knock at heaven's gate. And let us find contentment in the labor he gives us, though we may, like the prophets of old, only hope to see the newness that the coming of the Messiah shall bring.

10

NOT BECOMING WHAT YOU HATE

THE BIBLE EXHORTS US to "hate what is evil, hold fast to what is good" (Romans 12:9). In Ephesians 6 Paul urges us to stand strong in the battle against evil. Amos tells us that we are to "hate evil, and love good, and establish justice" (Amos 5:15). And so it appears that the Christian life will entail strong emotions about certain things. We will find ourselves reviling things, being disgusted with them and disdaining them. Scripture provides images of such responses, actions compelled by strong emotions, a hatred of evil. Jesus cleared the moneychangers and animals from the temple with whips. I cannot think of any word other than *hate* to adequately characterize his feelings about what he saw happening in his Father's house. Conversely, it could be said that his love for his Father's house, its purpose and integrity, compelled him. That is just the opposite side of the same coin, because this compelling love is what raises great indignation in Jesus and causes him to act so passionately against injustice. He appears to be very angry.

But it seems there are to be limits to our anger and restraints on our actions. In Ephesians 4:26 Paul says, "Be angry but do not sin; do not let the sun go down on your anger." And later in chapter 6 he tells us that "we are not contending against flesh and blood" (verse 12). So we may be angry, even in the community of faith (since that is the context of the

Ephesians 4 counsel) but we may not wallow in anger or nourish it. Other people—believers or not—are not our real enemies. And we may not act in vengeance (Romans 12:19).

Why these restraints? Why is the location of the evil we are to hate not in the actual person who is acting unjustly?

The answer lies in the falsehood of an old slogan: "The end justifies the means." The end never justifies the means. The means stand on their own merit. We would even do well to consider the end as inherent in the means.

The fact that God brought redemption for all of humanity from Jesus' betrayal and crucifixion does not make the acts of betrayal and crucifixion holy. Judas's death captures this for us. God will achieve the ends he desires, but we are called to be faithful in pursuing those ends by the means he prescribes. The reason is this: God knows that if we choose the means that our enemy chooses, we defeat him in a battle but he wins the war over our hearts and minds, for he has persuaded us to follow him and not the Lord. Though we may gain a temporary foothold, he has won the battle by a crafty outflanking maneuver.

Do you ever wonder why it is that after revolutionaries overthrow a repressive regime, they themselves become oppressive? Why is it that the means by which people gain power seem to determine how they will use it? Why do many political aspirants with idealistic intentions often end up repeating the moral failures of those who came before them? I suggest the answer lies in part in what it took for them to gain power, what shaped them as they sought political power.

God does not want us to use the enemy's methods to pursue kingdom results. This is very clear in Jesus' response to temptation in the fourth chapter of Luke. God wants us to use kingdom means to achieve kingdom ends. And his means have been shown most clearly in the life of his Son. Humility, sacrifice, service, love, joy, peace, patience, kindness, goodness, faithfulness, gentleness and self-control are all in play. Worship, fasting and prayer are powerful weapons. These all do great violence to the trends of the world. They are great weapons for a wider, more meaningful war.

When we get involved with real practical discipleship in justice work, we encounter a temptation to really hate the people who are committing the injustices or those who remain indifferent to the problem. Frankly, that kind of hatred is not Christian.

LOVE THY ENEMIES: CHRISTIAN SPIRITUALITY IN CONFLICT

Our participation in the bringing of the kingdom of God must be Christian in the means as well as the desired ends. We must not adopt the ways of the world in the name of accomplishing good ends. Scripture lays down several litmus tests of our spirituality in this regard. Love of enemies is one.

Jesus clearly commands, "Love your enemies, . . . pray for those who abuse you" (Luke 6:27-28). This is no small task. For in this pair of commands we are forced to recognize the humanity and dignity of those who act unjustly.

In the heat of the civil rights movement, Martin Luther King Jr. preached that those involved in the struggle must be interested not only in their own redemption, not only in their own salvation, not only in their own liberation, but also in the liberation of the policeman with the dog or the thug with the club. "When you come to love on this level, you begin to love [people] not because they are likable, not because they do things that attract us, but because God loves them and here we love the person who does the evil deed while hating the deed that the person does" ("A Testament of Hope," in *The Power of Nonviolence*, p. 13). His words challenge me. I believe King had read the words of Jesus and was seeking to live them and guide the movement with them.

Consider Fredrick Douglass's reflections on the effect that slavery had on one woman who owned him:

> Slavery proved as injurious to her as it did to me. When I went there, she was a pious, warm, and tender-hearted woman. There was no sorrow or suffering for which she had not a tear. She had

bread for the hungry, clothes for the naked, and comfort for every
mourner that came within her reach. Slavery soon proved its ability to divest her of these heavenly qualities. Under its influence, the
tender heart became like stone, and the lamb-like disposition gave
way to one of tiger-like fierceness. (*Autobiography of Frederick Douglass*, p. 63)

The injustice of slavery not only imprisoned slaves and treated them
inhumanely; it imprisoned the masters as well. It made them into what
they were not created to be. It taught them cruelty, when they had been
assigned kindness. It imprisoned them in greed, when they were born
for generosity. Through it they learned to care little for people who were
as eternal, as valuable, as they were. Through it they learned to care little
for their neighbor.

This does not absolve slaveholders of responsibility for their actions.
They were complicit in slavery's evil. But they were born in to a world
and a set of systems that did not train them well. Their education system
and families failed them. They did not have the opportunities they
needed. It was not a level playing field. They were as tortured, as lost, as
many slaves—maybe more so.

NOT BY ANY MEANS NECESSARY

Malcolm X once said that we should pursue our own defense and the establishment of just relations for the black community by any means necessary. He was an amazing leader, and I appreciate his strong emotions,
the feelings behind his words. I have felt the same rage at injustice and
the same impatience with what some call progress. I lived through the
1992 riots in Los Angeles, and though I didn't throw any bricks, I could
have. I understand the rage of those who were done with the Los Angeles
Police Department then. I understand the poverty and the regular indig-
nities that so many people in South L.A. have suffered from the police
and various government agencies over the years. I understand the disgust and violation people have experienced in our judicial system. But

though I understand and at times have felt drawn toward responses that are similar to those during that time of civil unrest, I have been restrained by the Lord's Spirit. As I have grown older and gotten a broader perspective about the widespread poverty and corruption around the world, I am amazed at the patient endurance of many believers. With the vision of the kingdom in their hearts, it is a miracle there is not more war.

Jesus gives us perspective: "My kingship is not of this world; if my kingship were of this world, my servants would fight, that I might not be handed over to the Jews; but my kingship is not from the world" (John 18:36). Paul adds in 2 Corinthians 10 that "though we live in the world we are not carrying on a worldly war, for the weapons of our warfare are not worldly but have divine power to destroy strongholds" (verses 3-4). Prayer, preaching, fasting and worship are real weapons in this battle, and they are only part of our arsenal as Christians. The violence we must confront as we do kingdom work is real, and we're called to fight it. But as we seek to be agents of the Lord in the world, we may not use any means necessary, and we may not resort to violent revolution.

Though we may—indeed we must—hate what is evil, and though we long for and labor for what is good, we may not pick up arms to establish the kingdom. The kingdom of God will not be established by armed conflict. There can be no Christian call to arms. Governing authorities and nations must promote good and restrain evil. They are to do so at times by force. But this is not the establishment of the kingdom of God. Jesus did not call his followers to fight in this way and did not even defend himself. The early church modeled their discipleship in this. Though I cannot call myself a pacifist, Jesus' model and Jesus' teaching are a restraint and a challenge to the spirituality of all of us who labor to love the poor and establish justice.

11

FINISHING THE RACE

IF WE ARE TO HAVE a sustainable life as we work for justice, we must seek a Christian spirituality that is balanced and not just focus on the elements that are oriented toward social justice. Christian spirituality is so rich and vast that to draw on only one aspect would leave us emaciated and ill-equipped for what we face in the world. We have a rich heritage of faith in Jesus; it contains all that we need to live in the world and minister in his name. But over the centuries of the church, divisions have alienated some elements of Christianity from one another. Some divisions have resulted from excesses in a church or denomination, but many times division is based on hostility toward what we are unfamiliar with. We would do well to be like the Beroeans (Acts 17), checking out what we hear and experience by seeking the wisdom of the Scriptures.

In *Streams of Living Water* Richard Foster identifies six streams of the Christian faith. I like his classifications and will take some time to describe them in my own words here. Consider getting Foster's book and reading it with care, since it presents the scriptural background and the history of each stream. It also includes case studies—a brief bio of one or two people from Christian history who exemplify each stream of spirituality.

We need a balanced spirituality because it is what Jesus exemplifies for us and calls us to. However, we also need each stream if we are to persevere in ministry. Though we don't know how long we have to live, we do know that we need to finish our days well. In order to have the vision, guidance, passion, strength, power, purity and love we need to live the Christian life, we need to draw water from all the streams of our faith. We need not try to put down buckets in all of them at once, but regular drinking from each stream will greatly benefit us and those we serve. This well-rounded spirituality will also give clarity and balance to our pursuit of justice work for the sake of the kingdom.

SOCIAL JUSTICE IS NOT ENOUGH

What you have read in the previous pages of this book arises from the social justice stream. It is focused on love for the poor, concern for justice and the transformation of society. It is strongly rooted in the corporate or communal righteousness arena. Due to the strong current of individualism in U.S. culture, American Christians tend to focus on personal justice and righteousness. Yet Scripture is concerned with both individuals and groups of people. Our cultural individualism tends to blind us to the biblical assumption of community.

American Christians have also tended to fear that those who pursue justice will not actually preach the Word to those they serve or may become lost in work that is only temporal. The current hostility toward Christianity partly has its roots in a relativistic tolerance. It will tolerate much except a claim to have absolute truth. Many fear that due to this, some will not speak about the gospel and only attend to social needs.

Such concerns are well founded. Some Christians working for justice have actually thrown out or forgotten about evangelism. People have become lost in relativism. But this is true regarding any one of the streams: if our spirituality is not balanced, serious dangers loom ahead, both for us and those we would seek to minister to. But tending to all dimensions of Christian spirituality helps bring balance, longevity, wisdom and power into the life of any believer, community of faith or ministry.

THE CONTEMPLATIVE LIFE

Prayer, silence, meditation and contemplation are central disciplines for this stream of the Christian faith. It appreciates the truth of Isaiah 64:4. In our world of busyness and scheduling, this is an often-neglected arena of spirituality.

There is always something more that could be done. There is always someone to visit, some injustice to address, some information to sift through, some book to read. The work that could be done will always be greater than the amount of time and energy we have. The advent of the Web, e-mail and cell phones has only increased the pressure to always be available and connected to other people. Relationally, some of us operate out of fear that if we disconnect we will miss something or be left out. Demands for immediate response are increasing in the world of business. There are real consequences if you are not quick enough: someone else will get the deal and make the money.

The disciplines of contemplative Christianity remind us of God's sovereignty, his work in the world that is beyond our efforts. They offer us the opportunity to be quiet in God's presence and recognize our dependence on him. They are means to receive the peace and strength we need for our work. They are the very personal side of Christian spirituality.

This element helps in justice work in a variety of ways. It centers us in the presence of God and reminds us of our need for his help. It reminds us that our human efforts are at best ineffective and at worst contribute to the problems. We need God to move. We need him to change other people. And we need him to change us as we seek to minister to others. Focusing us on the presence of God in and around us, the contemplative stream gives us perspective on the spiritual evil that is our real enemy.

THE CENTRALITY OF THE WORD

Foster calls this the evangelical stream of Christian spirituality. Here the word *evangelical* has a different resonance from the meaning attached to it within the broader culture. It points to a stream of spirituality that is very Word-centered, concerned with the proclamation of the gospel to others. This stream encourages and nurtures such disciplines as study and verbal evangelism, both personal and corporate. It focuses on the truth of God expressed in the Scriptures and on getting to know this truth thoroughly, declaring it to others and urging them to accept it. It also tends to focus us on the development of our minds and their transformation.

This stream's contribution to justice work is that it gives us wisdom about the worldly models and situations we face. This stream nourishes us with wisdom from the Word for our work and our lives. The Word is our barometer for examining ourselves, as well as institutions and policies we encounter. The Spirit of God can work through Scripture to enlighten, enliven and empower us.

A LIFE AND MINISTRY OF POWER

This stream has gained notoriety in recent years as the charismatic movement of the modern era. However, it goes back thousands of years. As with all of these streams of spirituality, what we discover in it is not something new at all. Though new to us, it is simply being dusted off for this generation of believers.

This dimension of Christian spirituality focuses on the ministry of the Holy Spirit and the gifts that Jesus offers to us through the Spirit. It appreciates the wisdom of God given in the moment and the power of God to heal and deliver people from evil spirits. This stream fosters an appreciation for the presence of God in a very tangible sense.

Some people are concerned with the aspects of this stream that are emotional or seem out of control. Our Western scientific worldview does not have much room for things that are not entirely explainable or controllable. God's Spirit works powerfully and accomplishes beautiful things among his people, but sometimes the charismatic style makes us nervous—especially if we are unfamiliar with God's works of power.

The church I grew up in did not introduce me to any kind of charismatic spiritual experience. In fact I didn't really know such things existed until I was well into my college years. Then I was suspicious for a while, thinking that most of what I saw and heard at charismatic churches was phony. Some of it was. But a few years down the line, I recognized that though sometimes charismatic experiences prove false, this is true of any type of Christian faith practice. Excess and human brokenness leak into all of our spiritual practices. So God worked in me to help me relax in the presence of charismatic manifestations and discern the good elements from the bad. I now have the pleasure of ministering in charismatic environments from time to time. It is powerful to lay your hands on someone as you pray and see God heal them.

The strength of this stream in our pursuit of justice is that it brings us in touch with the powerful presence and work of God. God is able to deliver people and places from evil in a very tangible way. He is able to heal. He is able to change situations by the work of his Spirit. He is able to give us powerful experiences of his presence and strengthen us. We will need all of the above as we seek justice.

THE NEED FOR HOLINESS

This stream is concerned with our character and the motives underlying our actions. It is marked by a strong desire for purity of motive, and one way of seeking purity is searching "the heart" and examining our motives. Our emotions and thoughts move us—they are the sources of our behavior. Basically, the holiness stream seeks to purify our actions through purifying the source of them. A concern for holiness in action will look to cleanse the heart and mind of any way that we have sinned or currently do not trust God.

At the beginning of the Methodist movement, the commitment to holiness was so serious that if you did not commit yourself enough to your reflection, prayer and repentance, your membership was revoked. You had to take confession and cutting off sin seriously, or others assumed you weren't really interested. Christian accountability, confession and real repentance are central to this theme of faith.

The holiness stream is essential for justice work if we hope to not become what we hate. If we actually hope to live lives of love and truth, purity of heart will be essential. If we hope to actually love our enemies, be patient with change and grow to be more like Jesus, we must continually seek the transformative power of the kingdom personally, lest we be co-opted by the powers that be.

PRACTICING THE PRESENCE OF GOD

This stream celebrates the possibility of knowing God in the common, everyday aspects of life. Our day-to-day routine can tempt us to forget about God. But the Lord is always with us and always present. The issue is whether we are always present to him—not just in times of powerful healing ministry, not just in our quiet time of meditation, not just in our study of the Word, not just in our confession and repentance with others, but in our normal routines of work and rest and play.

Some would call this sacramental living. It is the practice of the holiness and presence of God in all we do. We are challenged not to compartmentalize the faith or the presence of God to certain times and experiences. We are challenged to be present to God in all that we do, whether we are answering e-mail, peeling potatoes, playing basketball, eating dinner or changing the baby's diaper.

This stream helps us recognize God's presence and work in the small things. Much justice work is focused on a goal or a certain set of hoped-for results. The problem is that the goals never end and the results are frequently transitory. Sometimes our goals are also so large and long-term that we get worn out from the day-to-day work. We need to be able to celebrate the small things that are God's blessings and mercy to us each day. We need to recognize the small victories and the progress, however transient it may be. This stream protects us from an anxious need for results and helps us to focus on being rather than doing. It is of great help in the long haul to grow in our awareness of the presence and work of God in our mundane, everyday tasks. After all, much, if not most, of our life is actually spent on these kinds of tasks.

ALL IN ONE

Really what I have examined here are not six elements but rather a whole package of spirituality in one life—the life of Jesus. Though at a given time we may need to focus on one stream or another in order to learn from God and grow into greater maturity in the faith, all are ours and all should be integrated into our personal and corporate life. The goal is not to become a specialist in one stream but a believer who can draw on and be empowered by all that God offers us. Our faith communities should draw on them all. True Christian faith is a tough road, and we should be glad for all that we are given to help us make the journey successfully—not falling by the wayside or failing due to our stubbornness or short-comings.

A CLOSING WORD

I HOPE THAT THESE PAGES have nurtured your journey of faith. In many ways, they are a record of my own journey. The journey has taken me through various streams of the Christian faith and into a more integrated spirituality. It has taken me through seasons of working for social transformation, participating in powerful works of God, gaining a deep appreciation for Scripture, focusing on prayer and holiness, and now to a greater appreciation for sacramental living. Along the way, it has been my delight to see many friends gain a love for the social justice stream as well. Many have grown and given themselves to concern for the poor in the United States and abroad. Though all of us have struggled—or are struggling—through seasons of disillusionment, we labor on.

The most persistent temptation for those who seek to live a Christian life is simply to quit, because a real life of faith is difficult. It is painful. It is uncomfortable. There is real joy, peace and provision in following Jesus—these and many other blessings are part of the journey. But the real Christian life encompasses sorrow. It is a life of losing life, of giving it away in sacrificial service like the Master. And in so doing, we find the life of God strengthening us, giving us the peace, joy, provision and purpose we long for.

There are many ways to quit. You could choose to define the faith so narrowly that it is comfortable to you and simply affirms the way you are already living. Or maybe it affirms a way of living that is humanly achievable. You could associate only with people who are like you, through whom you receive no genuine challenge to grow and change. You could be seriously fatigued or injured and in pain and therefore simply drop the work. You could become so bitter, authoritarian or hostile as to kill any real possibility of relationship with others who do not see things as you do. You could choose to be divisive and rally people to your cause to defend yourself. You could seek to build a reputation (or protect one) for yourself or your organization as the central goal.

I have seen people choose all of these, and I have struggled with each of them myself at times. Yet though we struggle with such temptations and at times give in to them, they are not what Jesus and his followers in the early church chose. In his humanity Jesus did not choose these things. Though his early disciples were tempted and struggled with them, in the end they—with one exception—did not choose them.

The real, full Christian life has not so much been tried and found lacking; rather it has mostly been found difficult and left untried. So hang in there as God changes you. I hope and pray that you recognize the partners God gives you for the journey and the opportunities he offers you to be involved in his work. He has given us a rich spirituality and much good work to accomplish together. Let's claim the whole package and settle for nothing less.

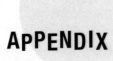

APPENDIX

THE FOLLOWING LIST of sources of information and resources for further study has been annotated to better direct your interest. They are all resources that others and I have found helpful in the journey.

THE BIBLE AND JUSTICE CONCERNS

Grigg, Viv. *Cry of the Urban Poor.* Monrovia, Calif.: MARC, 1992. 295 pages. On the severity of global poverty, the urbanization of poverty, who and where the poor are.

Linthicum, Bob. *Transforming Power.* Downers Grove, Ill.: InterVarsity Press, 2003. 216 pages. Biblical strategies for transforming neighborhoods.

McNeil, Brenda Salter, and Rick Richardson. *The Heart of Racial Justice.* Downers Grove, Ill.: InterVarsity Press, 2004. 187 pages. On inner transformation and social change as means of addressing a pernicious problem in the United States.

Myers, Bryant. *Walking with the Poor.* Maryknoll, N.Y.: Orbis, 1999. 279 pages. Some have found this helpful for evaluating development activity among the poor.

Perkins, John. *Restoring At-Risk Communities.* Grand Rapids: Baker,

1995. 266 pages. The basics of Christian community development. A good handbook.

Schlossner, Eric. *Fast Food Nation*. Boston: Houghton Mifflin, 2001. 356 pages. Scathing examination of this one trend in our nation and world and its effects on health, environment and income.

Sider, Ron. *Good News and Good Works*. Grand Rapids: Baker, 1999. 253 pages. On understanding the whole gospel and its implications.

THE SPIRITUAL ROOTS OF POVERTY, VIOLENCE AND OPPRESSION

Ellul, Jacques. *The Subversion of Christianity*. Translated by Geoffrey W. Bromiley. Grand Rapids: Eerdmans, 1986. 212 pages. From a social historian, tracing the evolution of the church's understanding of what it means to be a Christian.

————. *Violence*. Translated by Cecilia Gaul Kings. London: S.C.M. Press, 1970. 179 pages. The spiritual nature of violence and the power of love.

Sojourners magazine. Please see the periodical section below.

LIVING SIMPLY AND GIVING GENEROUSLY

Foster, Richard. *Freedom of Simplicity*. San Francisco: Harper & Row, 1981. 200 pages. Good practical guidelines for a more just and simple lifestyle.

Sider, Ron. *Rich Christians in an Age of Hunger*. 3rd ed. Dallas: Word, 1990. 261 pages. On the reality of world hunger, the U.S. economic situation and the effects of American lifestyle decisions on the rest of the world.

Wesley, John. *On the Use of Money*. London: Epworth, 1961. 15 pages. Good, hard, brief biblical instruction on the use of money.

INTERESTING TAKES ON AMERICAN HISTORY

Takaki, George. *A Different Mirror*. Boston: Back Bay Books, 1993. 428 pages. A treatment of U.S. history that gives attention to the roots and nurture of racism. Traces the Chinese, Irish, Black, Mexican and Native American histories in the United States.

Zinn, Howard. *A People's History of the United States.* New York: Harper Perennial, 1990. 582 pages. Relates a history of the United States from the viewpoint of people who have been exploited and who are seldom considered in more mainstream histories.

These two books are not liked by all historians, and they certainly do not say all that is to be said about American history, but they are useful to supplement more traditional writings. They fill out the picture. What is fascinating is to read these accounts side by side with teaching on biblical views of justice and right relations between people.

U.S. FOREIGN POLICY

Chomsky, Noam. *What Uncle Sam Really Wants.* Berkeley, Calif.: Odonian, 1992. 111 pages. Very brief book probing into some U.S. policy decisions and actions toward foreign governments.

Google these three things:

- "John Stockwell": Check out the info on the secret wars of the Central Intelligence Agency.

- "Bill Moyer, Secret Government"

- *School of Assassins:* A collection of video clips of former government officials and reporters speaking about many secretive operations that contributed to problems in other countries.

THE NEED FOR SYSTEMIC CHANGE

Kozol, Jonathan. *Savage Inequalities.* New York: HarperPerennial, 1992. 261 pages. On the inequalities in the educational system of the United States. He has other similar works in print.

Meggay, Melba. *Transforming Society.* Quezon City, Philippines: Institute for Studies in Asian Church and Culture, 1996. 108 pages. On the gospel's work among people to transform society in the Philippines.

A FULL CHRISTIAN SPIRITUALITY

Foster, Richard. *Streams of Living Water.* San Francisco: HarperSanFrancisco, 1998. 424 pages. Describes six streams of Christian spirituality, as examined briefly in chapter eleven of this book.

Tokunaga, Paul, ed. *Faith on the Edge.* Downers Grove, Ill.: InterVarsity Press, 1999. 204 pages. Comprehensive examination of Christian discipleship—looks at twenty-three different aspects in brief review.

PERIODICALS

Sojourners. http://www.sojo.net/index.cfm?action=magazine.home
A magazine highlighting justice issues in U.S. national life from a Christian perspective. Some Christians feel this magazine's perspective is a little extreme, but I have found some articles very helpful.

Prism. http://www.esa-online.org
A periodical put out by Evangelicals for Social Action that takes up justice concerns and trends in Christian spirituality.

Both of these magazines offer free e-mail newsletters as well as the print version.

NEWS SOURCES

If you like CNN, that's fine, just pepper your listening with some BBC and other news sources. National Public Radio is very worth listening to, though I find some of its programming and rhetoric too far left and/or non-Christian to be useful in discussion. It frequently does raise good questions and examines the news from a perspective that is absent from many major news sources. Evangelicals for Social Action is also a good information source on some issues.

http://www.cnn.com/
http://bbc.co.uk/
http://www.npr.org/
http://www.esa-online.org/

A FEW MINISTRIES TO CHECK OUT

If you are interested in some opportunities to serve in urban poor communities, check out the websites of the organizations below and explore the volunteer, internship, staffing and support options. Some organizations focus on domestic work and others are more international in scope.

Christian Community Development Association: http://www.ccda.org/
InnerCHANGE: http://www.crmleaders.org/ministries/innerchange
John M. Perkins Foundation for Reconciliation & Development: http://www.jmpf.org/
Mission Year: http://www.missionyear.org/
Servant Partners: http://www.servantpartners.org/
Servants to Asia's Urban Poor: http://www.servantsasia.org/index.asp
Word Made Flesh: http://www.wordmadeflesh.org/